St. Mary's
The Finest Church West of the Mississippi

Candice Chaloupka
and Suzanne Wright

St. Mary's: The Finest Church West of the Mississippi
Authors Candice Chaloupka and Suzanne Wright
Copyright © 2010 BHC Publishing

Cover design by Candice Chaloupka, BHC Publishing
Book design by Candice Chaloupka and Suzanne Wright, BHC Publishing
Copyedited by Suzanne Wright
Proof Readers: David A. Vanderah and Grace Mendez

All rights reserved.

No part of this book may be reproduced in any form or by any electronic or mechanical means, including information storage and retrieval systems, without permission in writing from the publisher, except by a reviewer who may quote brief passages in a review.

Articles from the Telegraph Herald printed with permission of Woodward Communications, Inc.

Sources from the Archives of St. Mary's Church printed with the permission of St. Mary's Church.

Sources from the Archives of St. Archdiocese of Dubuque printed with the permission of the Archdiocese of Dubuque.

Sources from the Archives of Sisters of Mount St. Francis printed with the permission of the Sisters of Mount St. Francis.

BHC Publishing, LLC, Dubuque, Iowa
http://ballyhoocreative.com

Printed in the United States of America

First Printing: July 2010

ISBN 978-0-9827772-0-6

Dedicated to the families who made St. Mary's Church of Dubuque
the "Finest Church West of the Mississippi"

Contents

Acknowledgements	vii
Authors' Notes	ix
Introduction	xiii
Holy Trinity Church	1
The Building of St. Mary's Church	6
Priests of St. Mary's	14
Inside St. Mary's	54
St. Mary's School	104
People of St. Mary's	134
The Closing	154
Last Mass	168
The Founding Families	190
Pew Rent	196
Bibliography	202
Sponsors	205

Acknowledgements

Anyone who has ever undertaken a project such as this one knows the amount of work involved and the help and support needed. This project would not have been possible without the assistance of a number of individuals. The authors would like to thank them for their generous support, encouragement, and availability, often on short notice!

Most importantly we would like to give thanks and praise to our Lord and Savior, through Him, all things are possible. He is the reason the church was built. We would also like to pay tribute to the founding members; without their dedication and sacrifices, St. Mary's Parish would not have existed.

Many heartfelt thanks to Jackie Williams, the wonderful lady who served the people of St. Mary's for 11 years. Without your ongoing help with providing access to the archives and your knowledge of the people, this book would not have been printed!

The following people also deserve many thanks for their gracious donation of time, talent, and resources:

- Sister Carol Hoverman, editor of *The Witness*
- Reverends Mark McGovern and Loras C. Otting, Archivists, Archdiocese of Dubuque

- Sister Veronica Bagenstos, OSF, Archivist, Mt. St. Francis
- David A. Vanderah, for reading the drafts
- Joe Ryan and the staff at Carlisle/Ryan Digital Services
- The teachers of St. Mary's
- The Sisters of St. Francis
- Annie Wertz
- Father Steve Rosonke
- Mary Nevans-Pederson, Telegraph Herald staff writer

We would like to thank the following individuals for donating the rights to use their beautiful photographs:

- Don Long, Jr.
- Ron and Jennifer Tigges
- Barb Ehlers

The businesses and individuals that provided financial support:

- American Trust & Savings Bank
- Dutrac Community Credit Union
- Behr's Funeral Home
- Jim and Kathy Conlon

And, finally, all those who shared their stories.

On a personal note, I would like to thank my husband, Scott, for believing in me, providing the resources I needed and for understanding when I was engrossed in writing and forgot to make dinner. To my children, Brianna, Sara, and Michael, for being quiet and letting mom work on the book!

Finally, to my cousin Suzie. Jackie Williams was the one person that made it possible to get the book started. Suzie is the one person who made finishing the book possible. It was an honor and a privilege to work with you. I am blessed that you are not just my cousin but also my friend and sister in Christ!

Authors' Notes

History has always been a passion of mine. I believe we need to know history — not just to avoid repeating mistakes but so we do not take for granted the sacrifices and decisions that others made before us. We are *where* we are and *who* we are today because of them.

If it wasn't for an intrepid group of Germans who were willing to risk their lives to take a long journey to a new and strange country, this book would not exist — St. Mary's Church would not exist.

My journey with St. Mary's began as a second grader at St. Mary's School. I attended the school through sixth grade; the first year it merged with St. Patrick's and became Downtown Catholic.

I received the Sacraments of Reconciliation, Holy Communion, and Confirmation before I left the Catholic Church as a teenager. I returned to the Catholic church and to St. Mary's, thanks in part to the support and encouragement of Father Ardel Barta just a few years ago.

During the summer of 2009, prior to the announcement that St. Mary's might close, my husband and I discussed practicality versus sentimentalism. We lived in Bellevue and, after almost three years of driving twenty-five miles for Mass, when gas prices were high, we made the painful decision to change membership to

St. Joseph's in Bellevue which was only two blocks away. It was a difficult decision as I have many memories of attending Mass at St. Mary's.

When I learned my spiritual home was going to close, I wanted to do what I could to preserve her history. At first, my goal was to gather as much information for my own satisfaction, but I realized others would want to know this history. Others would want to see the beautiful yet forgotten pictures that had been collecting dust in the archives — to have images to remember this beautiful church.

So I began to sorting through all the information I had obtained from Jackie Williams, the parish secretary. Then I began searching other sources for information. Finally I beseeched my cousin, Suzanne Wright, who had been in the publishing business for a number of years, and had already published a book, to help me.

There were many times during the writing of this book that I wanted to quit. I now know truly what a labor of love is: when what you are doing takes a lot of work but you love it anyway!

And so I leave you with this true labor of love, as a gift from one Christian, one Catholic, one member of St. Mary's Church, to another.

God's peace and blessings be with you all,

Candice Chaloupka

Writing a book about the house and people of God is an honor and a privilege. It saddens me that St. Mary's has been closed, but do not mistake the closing of this building as a shrinking of God's kingdom. He reigns supreme and in all things He will be glorified. We may not be able to see how the closing will bring about that glory. As people of faith it is our responsibility to stay vigilant for the day when God's plan shines forth.

I am blessed for having been given the chance to help with the creation of this book. Not many authors get a chance for a second book and even fewer get to do so with a person as great as Candice. She worked so hard at the research and principal writing that the success of this book should be credited to none but the Holy Spirit and she. Cousin, thanks for asking me to put my two-cents worth into the book.

Suzanne Wright

Forget the former things;
   do not dwell on the past.

See, I am doing a new thing!
   Now it springs up; do you not perceive it?
   I am making a way in the desert
   and streams in the wasteland.
         —Isaiah 43:18-19 NIV

Jesus is Presented in the Temple
Photo © 2010, Candice Chaloupka

Introduction

In the summer of 2009, the recommendation to close St. Mary's Catholic Church was shared with the parishioners. That November, Dubuque's Archbishop Jerome Hanus sent a letter proclaiming that the church would close sometime in the Spring of 2010. Gone would be the parish that began 161 years before (1849) when 40 families petitioned Bishop Mathias to build a German Catholic Church, to meet their spiritual needs in a language they could comprehend.

What follows is a collection of facts, images, and stories about the parish, the people, and the power of St. Mary's Church.

Quotes from individuals who shared their thoughts and reflections have been italicized and indented while newspaper articles and letters obtained from archives are in a font that gives an old typewriter look. When possible, images have been inserted near where they are referenced.

The information from this book was obtained from a variety of resources, including the archives of St. Mary Church, the Archdiocese of Dubuque, and that of the Sisters of Mt. St. Francis. Books published earlier by the Archdiocese have also been referenced as well as information obtained from individuals, though we have mostly relied on written documentation.

The information was consistent with the various sources with few exceptions. When there was an inconsistency with names or dates, we used the most commonly cited one.

Throughout the various media sources discussing the closing, a range of dates was used for how long the church was open; from 153 years to 161 years. This inconsistency comes from what was used as the founding date. Some have chosen to use when the current edifice was completed (1867), giving a 153–year-old history. Some counted from when the predecessor to St. Mary's was built, what is referred to as old Holy Trinity, completed in 1853. Finally, some refer to the date when German immigrants first petitioned to have a the old Holy Trinity Church built in 1849.

This book is not an exhaustive history so much as it is a grateful devotion to God for the priests, sisters, lay teachers, and parishioners who have impacted the lives of those in and around the parish.

As this book is a devotion and meant to commemorate St. Mary's and her people, the authors felt it would not be appropriate to make a profit.

We were fortunate to have so many people willing to donate their time and talent. We also sought out sponsors to help cover the initial printing costs, so please see the Acknowledgment and Sponsor sections of the book.

If, after covering costs of publishing and printing, there is money left over, it will be donated to the Sisters of St. Francis in Dubuque, Iowa, for their years of dedicated service.

We appreciate your support as well and pray you find the book all you had hoped it would be.

There is an appointed time for everything,
  and a time for every affair under the heavens.
A time to be born, and a time to die;
  a time to plant, and a time to uproot the plant.
A time to kill, and a time to heal;
  a time to tear down, and a time to build.
A time to weep, and a time to laugh;
  a time to mourn, and a time to dance.
A time to scatter stones, and a time to gather them;
  a time to embrace, and a time to be far from embraces.
A time to see, and a time to lose;
  a time to keep, and a time to cast away.
A time to rend, and a time to sew;
  a time to be silent, and a time to speak.
A time to love, and a time to hate;
  a time for war, and a time for peace.
  —Ecclesiastes 3:1-8 NAB

Holy Trinity Church
Contributed by St. Mary Church Archives

Holy Trinity Church

In 1849, forty German families petitioned Bishop Mathias Loras to build a German Catholic church in Dubuque, Iowa. At that time, St. Raphael's Cathedral served the immigrants from Ireland, Germany, and the Grand Duchy of Luxembourg. Bishop Mathias Loras recognized the spiritual needs of the families, who were for the most part without a good knowledge of English. He knew they could not be adequately cared for without the use of their native language for the sermons and instructions and so he granted the petition. (Schroeder, 1935)

H.V. Guilday drew up plans for what was to be dedicated as Holy Trinity Church. It was to be built in the German settlement known as "Five Points." The land, which was donated by the Hueckel family, was located on the corner of what is now Eighth and White Streets. (Kempker, 1853) The building was constructed using stones from many local home quarries. The building's design included a 20-foot high tower in front. (1962 and 2007 brochures)

"According to the May 11, 1851 *Weekly Miner's Express*, the festivities held for the laying of the cornerstone, involved music by the German band and a sermon by Sinsinawa's Father Samuel Mazzuchelli." (St. Mary's Archives) Bishop Loras "was very solicitous about having the church built, and when it was ready for the cornerstone, he went in procession from the Cathedral, north on Bluff, and then east on Eighth Street, and blessed the cornerstone with all solemnity." (Kempker, 1853)

Reverend George Plathe initially served as pastor for the new church. He was a missionary priest who also served other newly settled communities. Holy Trinity was appointed their first resident pastor on New Year's Eve, 1852, when the Reverend William Emonds was appointed by Bishop Loras.

The congregation rapidly outgrew the stone church. From 1853–1867, there were 2,733 baptisms. By 1863, there were over 300 official members. The German Roman Catholic Building Association was formed on April 13, 1863, to begin planning for a new, larger church building.

The following officers were appointed: President, Jacob Schmidt; Secretary, Adam Schaffner; Directors, Rudolph Nolte, H. Lembeck, H. Brinkman, and John Hartmann. These men were the original incorporators and practical financiers of St. Mary's Church. (St. Mary's Archives)

The Rock Church, Named Holy Trinity on Eighth and White Streets, Note: Front porch added after the building was no longer used as a church.
Contributed by St. Mary Church Archives

The group met monthly to raise the needed funds to build a new church to accommodate the increases in membership. The monthly gatherings lasted until the church was built in 1867. To motivate the members to give and do all they could for the erection of the new church, they adopted the motto: "The finest church west of the Mississippi River." (St. Mary Church Archives)

The original Holy Trinity Church building was converted to a commercial property. The last occupant was the Key City Roofing Company. The building remained in use until 1963 and was demolished in 1983. A plaque was erected to commemorate the original building. (Schroeder, 1935)

Plaque on Eighth and White Streets commemorating Holy Trinity Church,
Photo © 2010, Candice Chaloupka

Express & Herald

Wednesday Morning December 26, 1853

Osmond Roros was brought before the Police Court yesterday morning, charged with an assault with intent to commit murder, by firing a double-barreled shot gun loaded with slugs and buckshot, through the Southeast window of the Catholic Church, on the corner of Eighth and White Streets, on Christmas Eve, about 20 minutes past 12 o'clock.

Friday Morning December 28, 1853

Osmond Roros was arrested yesterday for disturbing public worship at the Catholic Church on Christmas Eve. This makes the third arrest of the individual. There is much excitement in regard to this case. The Court House was filled during the afternoon and evening. A jury was impaneled in the afternoon, and most of the time was passed in the examination of witnesses. The trial was still progressing up to the time we went to press.

Saturday Morning December 29, 1853

The case of Osmond Roros still continues to excite much interest. For the offence of disturbing public worship at the Catholic Church by firing a gun, the jury brought in a verdict of guilty. The accused was fined $50.00 and costs. A notice of appeal was given in this case.

The Prosecution of Osmond Roros — We believe the man who fired into the Church, no matter who it may be, ought to be severely punished, but it should also be recollected that prosecution if carried too far becomes persecution. We think Roros will be sufficiently punished for the outrage he is charged with committing if convicted of the charges already preferred. The penalty is severe, and the costs will be heavy.

Aerial View of Dubuque, 1800's
Contributed by St. Mary Church Archives

St. Mary's Church 1918
Contributed by St. Mary Church Archives

The Building of St. Mary's Church

Initially the parish board looked into buying the an existing church from the Presbyterians, located on Tenth and Locust Streets for the amount of $15,000. The building still stands and is known as the First Congregational Church of Dubuque. However, the Protestants "united and opposed" the sale. (Hoffman, 1938) Instead, the Langworthy Estate orchard, was purchased for $3,000.

John Mullany, an Irish architect who also designed St. Raphael's Cathedral, modeled the Gothic-styled design after the Salisbury Cathedral in England. The church measured 169-feet in length, 68-feet wide with a 73-foot ceiling. It had the tallest steeple in the city rising to a height of 252-feet.

> *In all justice to the Salisbury Cathedral, it must be mentioned that the only resemblance of the new church to the old was the tower and a hybrid species of florid Gothic style.* (Hoffman, 1938)

Building

The foundation was completed September 5, 1864, with $3.03 remaining in the treasury. The plans projected a cost of $80,000 to complete the church. Additional money was raised and the cornerstone was laid on August 25, 1865. The current building was erected over a three-year period with the parishioners themselves doing much of the excavation and construction. The total cost to build was $97,000. (Hoffman, 1938)

On February 10, 1867, Archbishop Hennessy dedicated the new church to St. Mary and was it was placed under the patronage of Our Lady's Assumption.

> *Only foundation space was dug out. After building was well along, then the cellar was dug. The parishioners spent many consecutive evenings digging. A track was built through chapel windows for dirt carts that were pushed out by youngsters such as Mr. Neuman. The various breweries would donate beer to the men, Heeb, Schmids and Tschirgi. The smaller boys would get a small glass.* (Neuman, 1943)

> *I had the opportunity to see the portion of St. Mary's basement that was never finished. I would estimate that area is probably 2/3 of the total area of the basement. There is still the ground floor and huge wooden pillars under each of the columns running down the inside of the church.* —Dave Becker (2010)

On September 27, 1943, Mr. Peter Hoffman interviewed Mr. Albert Neuman, born 1858, about his memories of St. Mary's Church.

> *When my parents with myself came to Dubuque from Ohio in 1855, there were three Catholic churches in the city. The first, St. Raphael's Cathedral, built of native stone, was erected in 1835 by Reverend Samuel Charles Mazzuchelli, on the site of the present St. Raphael School. The second, the old Holy Trinity Church, also a stone building, erected in 1851, on the corner of Eighth and White Streets, by the German Catholics in the city. The third, was the old St. Patrick's church, a frame building, on the corner of 14th and Iowa Streets, was built in 1853 or 1854.*

Neither of these churches exist today; all of them, in time, having been replaced on a different site by better and larger buildings. Until St. Anthony's was built some time during the 1870s, these were the only three Catholic churches in Dubuque.

The members of the stone church on Eighth Street, the old Holy Trinity Parish, were mostly all Germans or of German descent, who resided in all parts of the city. But most of them were in the north (now the center part) of the city.

From my earliest childhood I was an attendant of the old church. The parochial school of the parish was in the basement of the church, where German was taught in the forenoon and English in the afternoon. This is the school I attended until I graduated in 1868.

The membership of the parish increased very fast and by 1860, the church and school were too small. Therefore rooms in private residences were rented and used for school rooms, and preparations were made to build a new and larger church.

By 1863, $41,000 had been subscribed for the new church which when finished cost $97,000. The new church was built in 1865–66 (dedicated February 10, 1867) and was named St. Mary's Church, and the parish has since been called St. Mary's Parish.

After St. Mary's was built, the upper floor, the church floor of the old church, was converted into and used as a school until 1874. In 1874, St. Mary's School was built and the use of the old church was discontinued. But in 1878, it became the first residence of the newly arrived Sisters of St. Francis who occupied it until October 1879, after which time the [old] church was sold.

I was born and baptized in Dayton, OH, but all of my brothers and my only sister were born in Dubuque. My brothers were baptized in the old Holy Trinity Church, but the younger, my sister Mary, and brother Dominick (Nick) were baptized in St. Mary's.

Myself and brothers Matt, Frank, and John attended school in the old Eighth Street building, but Nick, the youngest, attended school at St. Mary's and St. Joseph College (Mary died before she was old enough to go to school).

Myself and all my brothers received their First Communion at St. Mary's. I was a member of the First Communion class of St. Mary's in May 1867. (St. Mary's Church Archives)

Names of the members of the old Holy Trinity Parish can be found in the "People of St. Mary's" chapter.

St. Mary's Church 2009
Photo © Candice Chaloupka

DUBUQUE DAILY HERALD

Sunday, April 24, 1864   Page 4

The New German Catholic Church

Active preparations for the building of the German Catholic Church have been progressing for some time past, and the time is now rapidly approaching when ground will be broke and the work commenced.

Last summer ground was purchased on White Street between 15th and 16th Streets for the erection of the edifice. It comprises five lots and is as convenient and good a location as can be found in any part of the city. John Mullany, so long and favorably known in the city, was selected as the architect and will have the superintendence of the construction. His plans have been submitted to the church authorities and been accepted and work will be commenced the first Monday in May.

The structure is to be of brick, 140 by 68 feet, and will be of the Gothic style of architecture. The tower will be 290 feet in height. The church will front upon 15th Street, and when completed will meet a thousand people. It will cost altogether $25,000, and will be a decided ornament to the city.

The mason work for the foundation has been let to Martin Pfiffner and Bro., who will commence their work next week and have contracted to have it done by the first of September. The society has already paid for their lot, have enough on hand to more than pay for the foundation and leave a balance for the erection of the building.

It is the design to proceed only as they are able to pay so that when completed there will be no burdensome debt hanging over them. It will probably be two or three years before the church will be ready for occupancy, but when so it will be just what would be desired — a fine building, finely situated and all paid for.

Dubuque Daily Herald

Tuesday, May 10, 1864   Page 4

Breaking Ground for the New Catholic Church

The ceremonies of breaking ground for the erection of the new Catholic Church at the corner of White and Fifteenth Streets, took place yesterday.

Owing to their being no announcement in the papers of the event, there was but a small attendance, but enough to inaugurate the commencement of the building.

Rev. Father Walsh was present and with a spade broke the ground on which is to stand the edifice. After a few appropriate remarks, the excavation for the foundation commenced and was vigorously pushed forward during the day.

As the society has to excavate its own foundation, all those who are idle or have time to spare can lend a hand to the cause by applying on the ground.

DUBUQUE DAILY HERALD

Saturday, October 13, 1866   Page 4

Sad Accident: A Workman Falls from a Steeple, Seventy Feet High and Is Killed Instantly

A terrible accident took place at st. Mary's Church on the 12th inst., which has struck a chill to many hearts and plunged a happy family in the deepest gloom. A young man, twenty-four years of age, by the name of Michael Neylan while working on the spire of the church at a distance of seventy feet from the ground, lost his footing and was precipitated to the floor below.

The unfortunate man struck upon his head and was killed instantly. It appears that he was standing upon a light staging near the center of the steeple hoisting timber, when the tie beam gave way and he fell a distance of ten feet and struck a two inch board which broke with his weight. Had this been strong enough, the man's fall would have been checked.

The fall to the second staging was forty feet, and here he struck upon another board which tipped up and allowed him to fall the whole distance. He was probably killed before he reached the ground as he never breathed or moved.

He was a quite industrious young man of most exemplary habits. He was a carpenter by trade and resided with his parents at the corner of Twelfth and Washington Streets. Two weeks ago he took out a policy from Kniest and Williams, agents for the Chicago Accident Insurance Co., for fifteen hundred dollars, the amount of his premium for the same being only nine dollars. This money, as soon as the proper certificates of his death are forwarded, will be promptly handed over to his parents, and illustrates fully the benefits to be derived from accident or life insurance.

It is certainly a sad affair, and happened in a singular manner. The aperture through which he fell was only three feet six inches wide, and he broke three different scaffolds. Mr. Mullany, the contractor was standing on the exact spot where he fell, a few moments before, and had he not stepped away, would probably have lost his life. Men employed in such situations cannot exercise too much caution in guarding against accident.

Rev. William Emonds, First Resident Pastor (1852–1855)
Photos on this page contributed by St. Mary Church Archives

Rev. Aloysius Meis
Pastor (1864–1871)

Rev. John Fendrick
Pastor (1860–1864)

Priests of St. Mary's

The first permanent pastor appointed by Bishop Loras to Holy Trinity Church (St. Mary's) was Father William Emonds. He was appointed on New Year's Eve, 1852, after having been ordained by Bishop Mathias Loras only a few days before this appointment. Eager to get started in his new life as a priest, he celebrated the first mass with his new congregation the day after his appointment on January 1, 1853. Reverend Emonds began his ministry serving not only Holy Trinity but also the churches in Sherrill's Mound, north of Dubuque, and St. Catherine's to the south of Dubuque. He served St. Mary's until 1855 when he was transferred to Iowa City.

Over the next decade, four different pastors served this fledgling parish: Reverend Matthew Lentner (1855–856), Reverend Nicholas Felderman (served four months in 1856), Reverend George Schneider (1856–860), and Reverend John Fendrick (1860–1864).

Very little is known about these priests or why there were so many changes in leadership in a short time. These changes did not stop Holy Trinity Parish from growing. During Reverend Fendrick's tenure the members of Holy Trinity organized the German Roman Catholic Building Association of Dubuque. The group first met on

April 13, 1863, and their mission was to plan the building of a new church to accommodate the rapidly growing congregation.

Reverend Aloys Meis took over duties in 1864. During his time as pastor, the new church building began. The cornerstone was laid on August 25, 1865 and the building was completed in 1867. The rectory and convent were also built during Reverend Meis' tenure. He served until 1871, when he was transferred to Fort Madison.

Convent
Contributed by St. Mary Church Archives

Rectory
Contributed by St. Mary Church Archives

Reverend Clement Johannes

Reverend Clement Johannes was appointed to replace Father Meis in 1871. St. Mary's made its greatest progress both in size and organization during his time as pastor. During his tenure, the Jackson Street School was built (1872) and the St. Mary's Casino was built in 1900–1901. The "Casino" became the center of social and educational activities for the parish as well as Catholic life in general in Dubuque. Built on the corner of 16th and White Streets, the Casino was a spacious center for meetings of societies and recreation facilities including bowling and billiards, kitchen, dining room, gymnasium, and calisthenics room. It also included a "real theatre with horseshoe balcony and seating capacity for 700." (Sigwarth, 1967)

The Casino, 16th and White Streets
Contributed by St. Mary Church Archives

Very Rev. Clement Johannes, Pastor (1871–1905)
Contributed by St. Mary Church Archives

On July 4, 1876, the Rockdale area, south of Dubuque, was flooded due to strong rain. Many people lost their lives in the tragedy.

> *At St. Mary's Church, a sorrowful scene was presented this afternoon. Five of the Peter Kapp family and six members of the John Klassen family rested upon their biers side by side while Father Johannes delivered an eloquent and impressive funeral sermon, most vividly depicting the horrid manner in which their lives paid tribute to the fury of the relentless storm. The funeral was largely attended and an immense procession followed their remains to the German Catholic Cemetery.* (Sigwarth, 1967)

Father Johannes died August 9, 1905, in the rectory and was buried August 14th.

DUBUQUE DAILY HERALD

Thursday, August 10, 1905

Father Clement Johannes Dead: End comes at 10:30 Wednesday after Lingering Illness

Funeral Will Be Monday: Last Rites for Beloved Priest at St. Mary's at Nine-thirty A.M.

Rev. Clement Johannes, irremovable rector of St. Mary's Roman Catholic Church, died at St. Mary's parsonage last night at 10:30 o'clock. His death was not unexpected for he had been sinking rapidly for the past few days.

The ill health of the well-beloved priest dates back four years, though it became serious only as many months ago, when he suffered a paralytic stroke which finally resulted in his death.

The demise of Father Johannes removes from the church a conspicuous figure. His achievements were such as to render him of much more than local prominence, as will be attested by the large number of priests who will be here from outside the archdiocese of Dubuque.

Rev. Clement Johannes was the son of Bernard and Catherine Johannes and was born in Germany in 1855. The first sixteen years of his life were spent in the fatherland, but in 1854 he came to America, landing at New Orleans. He came to Dubuque almost directly by steamer and remained until the following spring.

Then he left for Louisville, KY., where he studied for three years and thence going to Milwaukee, lived there six years. He attended the St. Francis Seminary in that city, graduating in 1868.

Bishop Hennig of Milwaukee ordained him that year and he was sent to Keokuk, Ia., where he was in charge of St. Mary's parish for fourteen months. He was then transferred to West Point, Lee County, Ia., and remained there two years.

In 1871 he was placed in charge of the cure with which he remained until his death, thirty-four years later. He is survived by one brother, August Johannes of Dyersville, by one sister, Mrs. Joseph Leuck of New Vienna, and by a sister-in-law, Mrs. Anna Johannes, also of New Vienna. Several nephews and nieces also mourn him.

Funeral will be Monday

Commencing Friday morning, the remains will lie in state in the chapel of St. Mary's Church and will be transferred to the church. The obsequies begin at 9:30 Monday morning, when the office for the dead will be chanted. The solemn requiem mass will be said about 10 a.m., after the chanting.

The funeral arrangements are not complete as yet and more details can not be announced until Friday.

His Life Work

Father Johannes's chief popular reputation was gained in connection with the establishment of St. Mary's orphan asylum, conducted by the Franciscan Sisters, who came here from Iowa City through his agency. Yet his work as rector of St. Mary's parish is the brightest diadem in the crown of achievement he justly wore. He leaves to mourn him and to mourn him long and sincerely a parish which is second to none in the state. [text missing] equipment, of buildings, it is the foremost in the city, and above all , in regard to its spiritual life, it is surely unexcelled. Largely at least through the conduct of the parish by the decedent, its people are as one big family.

The orphan asylum was founded with funds left for that purpose by Sennes Huegel, but a very large part of the big sums expended on it was given out of his private fortune by Father Johannes.

He also gave largely to the construction of St. Mary's Casino, the finest parish building in the state of Iowa. It is commonly understood that he also gave a sum to be used after his death for the erection of a funeral chapel in Mount Calvary Cemetery.

Tributes to the Dead Priest

The first general knowledge of his death came from the solemn tolling of the church bells at midnight. This morning the news was widely discussed and the fact of his demise universally lamented.

Below are a few of the many tributes to him which have been expressed:

During his pastorate, covering 35 years, he was never a Sunday away from his flock except when in the spirit of obedience he accompanied the late lamented Archbishop Hennessy to Rome. He believed that all his time belonged to God and his people. No wonder they idolized him as a devoted father.

His spirit of charity was as broad and deep as was his spirit of labor. Selfishness was to him a vice unknown; altruism had grown to be his second nature. But all his charities were done according to the injunction of the Savior: 'Let not thy left hand know what thy right hand had doeth.' He imposed silence as a condition upon the recipients of his benefactions. The widow and the orphan found in him a kind, generous father. In his demise the children of St. Mary's Orphanage have lost their best friend and greatest benefactor.

Reverend Heer

Rt. Reverend Monsignor George W. Heer, Pastor (1905–1928)
Contributed by St. Mary Church Archives

Rev. Heer, previous pastor of Dyersville Church for 18 years, took over as pastor when Father Johannes died. During his tenure, the parish continued to grow. In 1906, the Brothers of Mary from St. Louis were invited to come to Dubuque and with their help, the St. Mary's High School for Boys was opened. The high school was popular with the public and business owners; the graduates were easily able to find employment. After 22 years, the high school was closed and the building used to house students of the grade school.

The Immaculate Conception Academy for girls was opened in 1907 and located on 17th and Iowa Streets. The building still stands on what is now called Heeb Street and is now the "Power of Prayer" where 24 hour, seven–day-a-week, Eucharistic Adoration is held (at time of printing).

Father Heer was also a promoter of the German Catholic Central Verein, a federation of German Catholic Societies. They held a regional convention in Dubuque in 1907. It was a large event, bringing many dignitaries including the Rt. Rev. Diomede Falconio, the Papal Delegate who later became a Cardinal; Archbishop Messmer of Milwaukee; Bishop Schwebach of LaCrosse, WI; Joseph Matt, editor of the Wanderer of St. Paul; and Dr. Bitter, eminent member of the Catholics of Germany.

A parade was also part of the festivities which were described in one of the local newspapers:

> *The parade promises to be the most imposing ever witnessed in Dubuque, when between six and seven thousand men will be in the line of march accompanied by fifteen bands. The city will be in holiday attire and one of the largest crowds ever assembled within her gates is expected here on that day.* (Sigwarth, 1967)

St. Mary's Drum & Fife Corp
Contributed by St. Mary Church Archives

Father Buholt, assistant, had the fife and drum corps lead a caravan of horse drawn surreys from the depot as they escorted the papal delegate through the streets of the city. (Sigwarth, 1967)

Rome bestowed him with the distinction of a Protonotary Apostolic in 1912. The mass celebrating this honor was preached in German and English. A banquet in his honor was held at the Dubuque Club.

During Monsignor Heer's tenure World War I broke out and, in reaction, German textbooks were removed from the school and German sermons became less frequent, except at the high mass. (Sigwarth, 1967)

The last addition made to St. Mary's before Monsignor Heer retired was the installation of the marble altar for the Blessed Mother. The marble came from Italy and the mosaic depiction of the Mary of the Angels came from Munich. Monsignor Heer was unable to celebrate mass at this new altar due to his failing health. He retired as pastor in August of 1928 and died December 18, 1929.

Monsignor Heer, Father Smith with Communion Class, Year unknown
Contributed by St. Mary Church Archives

Reverend Zeyen

Rt. Reverend Monsignor Joseph J. Zeyen, Pastor (1928–1947)
Contributed by St. Mary Church Archives

The second week of September 1928, Reverend Joseph J. Zeyen transferred from Alta Vista, Iowa, to become the new pastor of St. Mary's. Father Zeyen had served as an assistant to Monsignor Heer from 1912 to 1915, so he was not a stranger to the parish.

Father Zeyen's tenure was during tough economic times for St. Mary's and all of Dubuque. Banks failed and there were many poor in the city. Father Zeyen saw to the needs of the people and fed the crowds that came to the back door of the rectory. Students fell asleep during class because they did not have breakfast so Father Zeyen bought milk for them. Long before the government began a hot lunch program, Father Zeyen began providing free hot lunch for the children who could not afford it.

The financially lean years did bring a spiritual awakening and many organizations flourished at the church including the St. Vincent De Paul Society, the Holy Name and Rosary Societies, Third Order of St. Francis, the Boy Scouts, and the first parish troop of Girl Scouts in the City.

> *We lived at the top of North Main and Heeb Streets by Madison Park (then known as Seminary Hill). I would go to the morning requiem masses for the dead on weekdays, before school. Even my parents went to daily mass. My father said, 'if Howard (my Jesuit brother) can do that, then I can go to daily mass.' My mom was involved in the Rosary Society and my dad in the Holy Name Society. During Lent, we did the Stations of the Cross every day after mass. My dad always led the prayer before meals. During Advent we always prayed the rosary every night. We had a Mary shrine in our home and we would all kneel around it to pray the rosary in May.*
> —Sister Marie Therese Kalb (2010)

Father Zeyen was also known for his singing as he often sang with the choir which boasted a full-voiced mixed group. St. Mary's was known for its great choirs and choir masters. One of the celebrated choir masters was Mathias Knippel who took over in 1924 and was the owner of the Church Goods House, a religious store still opened today as Knippels Religious Store. In 1929, William Keller took over as choir master and served "till the end of the great choir era in the forties." (Sigwarth, 1967)

In 1934, during the era of economic depression, the St. Mary's Credit Union was formed. Many were concerned it would become another Vincent de Paul Society, but those fears were unfounded. The Union began small but "thrift, responsibility, and concern for neighbor were virtues that grew with the growth of the Credit Union." (Sigwarth, 1967)

It was a success and in 1967, it boasted over 1800 members with assets reaching a high of one million, three hundred thousand dollars. Also during that year it was the largest church credit union in Iowa. St. Mary's Credit Union closed in 1990 and is now Dutrac Community Credit Union.

During the summer of 1935, Father Zeyen hosted a reunion for priests who studied at the Jesuit Seminary in Innsbruck, Austria. A pontifical mass was held as part of the celebration with Archbishop Beckman celebrating and Father Flanagan of Boy's Town preaching. The reunion was attended by 97 priests and the attendants were kept busy with meetings, banquets, social gatherings, and a river excursion.

The publication of a Sunday Bulletin was started by Father Zeyen, "The Bells of St. Mary's", was first begun on January 5, 1941.

Another tradition during the time of Father Zeyen was the Forty Hour Devotions. Society members associated with the church would gather to pray and sing in public adoration of the Eucharist. On the closing night of the devotions, the priest marched in procession along with dozens of acolytes followed by the laity with up to 50 visiting priests in attendance.

> During 40 Hour Devotion, the sister decorated the altar with red roses and vigil lights. The steps around the altar were covered with white sheets. Each day the candles were in a different formation to spell words. One day might be "Ave," the second day "IHS." There was a procession with the monstrance on the last night of the devotion. The altar boys wore the cassock and the children receiving the Sacrament of Holy Communion would wear their communion outfits. The children would join the priest in the procession through the church. Priests from other parishes would attend too.
> —Sister Marie Therese Kalb (2010)

Archbishop Beckman offered the honor of Monsignor to Father Zeyen in the thirties, but he refused. But on April 4, 1946, Father Zeyen was made a Monsignor.

Monsignor Zeyen died July 14, 1947. His funeral mass was offered by his nephew, Reverend Raymond Zeyen, a professor of music at St. Francis Seminary in Milwaukee. Right Reverend J. Fred Kriebs, manager of *The Witness*, preached, saying "Monsignor

Zeyen's name was accepted in the community as synonymous with charity." Known as a traveler and a man of ideas, it was said of him that "he put more living into a day than some did in a week." (Sigwarth, 1967)

Chaplain Aloysius Schmitt, LTJG (CHC)

Chaplain Aloysius Schmitt, LTJG (CHC), Assistant Pastor (1937–1939)
Contributed by St. Mary Church Archives

Chaplain Schmitt, Father Zeyen and Students, year unknown
Contributed by St. Mary Church Archives

I was in second grade when Father Schmitt died. My brother Jack's birthday is December 7 and he was having a party with his friends when our dad announced "we are at war."—Sister Marie Therese Kalb (2010)

Chaplain Aloysius Schmitt was born December 4, 1909, in St. Lucas, Iowa. An assistant Pastor to St. Mary's, he was one of the many Dubuque boys who went off to fight in World War II.

He started his tour of duty on June 28, 1939, serving as chaplain aboard the USS Oklahoma. On December 7, 1941, the Navy base in Pearl Harbor, Hawaii, was attacked by the Japanese. The USS Oklahoma was one of the ships damaged by Japanese Type 91 aerial torpedoes.

The attack on Pearl Harbor started after he finished celebrating the morning mass. During the attack, Chaplain Schmitt attended to the wounded on the ship's sickbay. When the ship was struck and started to take on water, he and the other men in the sickbay were trapped.

Chaplain Schmitt and some other men were able to find a compartment with small porthole to escape through. Schmitt began helping other men out the porthole to safety. As he began crawling through himself, he became aware of others that had entered the compartment. He came back to help the others, giving up his chance to escape as water was rapidly filling the compartment. Many of the crew members trapped were cut free by other sailors and civilian navy yard employees, but despite their best efforts, over 400 of her crew perished.

Chaplain Schmitt was one of the many who died that day. He and another chaplain, Chaplain Capt. Thomas Leroy Kirkpatrick, were the first chaplains to die in World War II.

It is said that Chaplain Schmitt saved the lives of twelve men before the ship sank. His name is engraved in the Courts of the Missing and he was posthumously awarded the Navy and Marine Corps Medal and Citation.

In 1943, a destroyer named USS Schmitt was commissioned by the Navy in his honor and served until 1967. Loras College in Dubuque dedicated the Christ the King Chapel in his memory and displays some of his property including his chalice and missal open to December 7, 1941.

A plaque was purchased by St. Mary's in 1943, and hangs on one of the pillars facing the people honoring this hero of World War II.

The city of Dubuque honored their hometown hero too; Chaplain Schmitt Island was named after Aloysius and is the home of the city's Veterans' Memorial Plaza, dedicated in 2009.

Chaplain Aloysius Schmitt, LTJG (CHC), Assistant Pastor (1937–1939)
Contributed by St. Mary Church Archives

Chaplain Schmitt Memorial Plaque
Photo © 2009, Don Long, Jr.

The memorial plaque purchased by St. Mary's Church reads as follows:

> *While serving on the U.S.S. Oklahoma he gave his life in the act of saving twelve of his shipmates at Pearl Harbor — Dec. 7, 1941. A grateful country awarded him posthumously the Navy and Marine Corps Medal and Citation. May he rest in peace.*

Monsignor Klott

Rt. Rev. Monsignor Joseph J. Klott, Pastor (1947–1956)
Contributed by St. Mary Church Archives

Monsignor Joseph Klott succeeded Monsignor Zeyen. He was the head of the Loras College Endowment Fund and was able to enrich it even during the Depression. He remained in charge of the fund even when he became pastor of St. Mary's.

During his tenure, St. Mary's transitioned from the traditional choir music sung in the loft to the Gregorian chants and participation of the congregation. "St. Mary's became truly a singing parish fifteen years before the changes instituted by Second Vatican Council." (Sigwarth, 1967).

Music was not the only change Monsignor Klott oversaw; after 40 years, it was necessary to renovate the interior of the church. Twice before, the walls, mural, and mosaics had been restored, but time marches on and once again, the congregation was faced with a decision: go modern or restore the past. St. Mary's had been a historical landmark with a rich history — the past would be reproduced.

The John C. Kaiser Company was given the responsibility of renovating the many works of art contained within the walls of St. Mary's Church.

Gold-leafed Altar
Photo © 2009, Candice Chaloupka

On the evening of January 13, 1956, while conversing with his assistant, Father Rahe, Monsignor Klott, "rose from his chair, stepped out of the room, came back and leaned against the door frame to announce that he was not feeling well, then tumbled and died as he was being anointed." (Sigwarth, 1967)

Monsignor Klott had performed his double duty as pastor and secretary of the Loras College Endowment Fund admirably. He left the parish treasury with $134,000 along with $22,000 of his own money that he willed to St. Mary's.

> *I helped out at St. Mary Parish for a surprisingly long time. Here is what happened. Msgr. Joseph Klott was pastor of St. Mary in the 1950s. At some point during the last year of his life, he asked me to offer a Mass each Sunday at the parish. Msgr. died suddenly January 16, 1956. Msgr. Sigwarth became the new pastor and he asked me to continue offering a Sunday Mass at the parish. This I did until he retired. At the same time I retired as President of Loras College. Msgr. Sigwarth asked if I would be able to take over as the new pastor. I had been president for seven years, and the load had been pretty heavy. While I appreciated Msgr. Sigwarth's confidence in me, I chose to serve a smaller parish — St. Joseph in Elkader. I always enjoyed my relationship with St. Mary's Parish, and am happy to have served there during the entire period of Msgr. Sigwarth's term, a truly fine and wonderful pastor.* —Msgr. Friedl (2010)

Reverend Sigwarth

Rev. Anthony W. Sigwarth, Pastor (1956–1977)
Contributed by St. Mary Church Archives

St. Mary's for me was Father Anthony Sigwarth. He was the pastor the entire time I was there. He had a great interest in the school and the children. He was a great mentor. He especially took an interested in the poor families.

When Father Sigwarth was the associate priest he was also the volleyball coach. The team practiced during recess and one year the school team was the champions in the school tournament. —Sister Corinne Kutsch (2010)

Reverend Anthony W. Sigwarth arrived on February 20, 1956, from Holy Cross, Iowa, to take over where Monsignor Klott left off. He had previously served as an assistant too and so was familiar to St. Mary's parish.

Reverend Sigwarth was a part of many changes to St. Mary's and the community of Dubuque. Changes to the Mass and layout of the physical church were implemented during his service as a result of Second Vatican Council. He was also the priest during the 100th year anniversary of the building of St. Mary's.

Ecumenically speaking, during the 1960s the Dubuque Council of Churches, comprised of three parishes in Dubuque's "underprivileged area — St. Mary's, Immanuel Congregational and St. John's Lutheran — spearheaded a movement which resulted in the establishment of the Washington Opportunity Center under the Economic Opportunity Act." (Sigwarth, 1967)

It became very evident that St. Mary's as a parish might suffer the same fate as have many inner city parishes in the country. Highways, industries, parking lots, and "what have you" were ready to invade the area of St. Mary's. When neighborhood meetings were called, it was found that strong neighborhood spirit still existed. This was an asset to work with and was encouraged.

As a result, the Washington Neighborhood Council was organized. A federally funded Opportunity Center became its first product. The building in which it was housed was leased at $1.00 a year from the Archdiocese of Dubuque. It is located at 12th and White Streets. (St. Mary's Archives, 1976)

The council also petitioned the city to rezone the area to as residential since 85 percent of the land was used as residential. Sixty-nine percent of the residents signed the petition and the City Council rezoned the area, exempting existing businesses and industries.

The ordinance was contested and ultimately appealed to the Supreme Court of Iowa; it was approved and reinstated. Strong leadership also diverted a proposed freeway which was moved further east, closer to industry and the river.

The Washington Neighborhood Free Tool Library also opened in a vacant storefront located on 17th and Jackson Streets. A wide variety of tools were available free of charge, donations accepted, to residents of the neighborhood.

> *We lived around the corner from the Tool Library, on Washington Street. My father owned a triplex and was always making repairs. He often sent me to the tool library to get what he needed.*
> —Candice Chaloupka (2010)

Another issue the Reverend Sigwarth spearheaded was the installation of traffic diverters (round-about) along Washington Street. Heavy truck traffic disturbed the peace of residential living so a campaign to route the heavy trucks along a designated truck route began and was successful. The traffic diverters became park-like attractions, with shrubs and flowers, enhancing the look of the area. (St. Mary's Archives, 1976)

> *I still have the original TH article, full page, from November 11, 1975, that gave him [Monsignor Sigwarth] credit for his challenging the city on many issues.*
>
> *During the time I was teaching in the "blue" school, Monsignor Sigwarth, along with Hank Waltz, got the city to put in the traffic diverters on Washington Street. That was because when the trucks going to the Packing House were so loud as they passed school that we had to stop teaching until they were gone by. No more trucks of pigs, etc., gave us the blessing of "quiet."*
> —Sister Carolyn Thirtle (2010)

[Sister Carolyn Thirtle was known as Sister Mary Edith Ann when she was teacher at St. Mary's from 1959–1966.]

> *I grew up near one of the round-a-bouts and they had signs that said "No Semis." A couple times a year a semi would drive around the circle. The "No Semi" sign would end up bent in half. It made quite a racket!*
> —Candice Chaloupka (2010)

Washington Neighborhood Resource Center
Photo © 2010, Candice Chaloupka

Washington Street Traffic Diverter (Round-about)
Photo © 2010, Candice Chaloupka

In 1967, St. Mary's celebrated its centennial. To commemorate the prior 100 years of this great church, Reverend Sigwarth compiled the history of St. Mary's and had it published into a 72-page book titled "Centennial Brochure." It was released to the public October 29, 1967. Much of the history for this book was obtained from this wonderful keepsake.

The centennial was observed on October 29, 1967, at 4 p.m. Five priests who formerly served at St. Mary's were speakers at the celebration dinner. The theme of the dinner was "A Bit of Reminiscing" and was held in the school hall.

The following is the homily given by Father Friedl in honor of the Centennial:

One hundred years ago, a congregation much like the one assembled today knelt in these pews, while the Bishop of the diocese and a group of priests, not unlike those who are in this sanctuary, blessed and dedicated this church. We have gathered on the great feast of Christ the King to reflect upon that distant event, to express our joy and thanks to God for the century just completed. And we signify this gratitude by offering to God His divine Son in a Eucharistic Sacrifice of thanksgiving.

We thank God, in the first place, for this church building, this magnificent house of God, which has for a hundred years brought such splendor to the prayer life of St. Mary's parish. While it is true that God is present in every place, yet throughout all of human history men have felt the need to contact God in specific locations. They would assemble to pray to Him before the Ark of the Covenant, in the temple of Jerusalem, in the synagogue, and in the church. And when Christ willed to become present among men in the form of the Eucharist, the church building became more than a place of assembly; more than a symbol of God's presence. It became in a genuine sense His home, His tabernacle, His dwelling place.

Yet, hallowed as this church building might be, our thoughts turn today to people, rather than to structures;

and we express our gratitude for the rich blessings which God has given without reserve to this parish, to this Christian family of the people of St. Mary's.

The blessings of God do not come from a single mold. They take many forms and so every parish seems to have its own special, identifying features, which make it different from every other parish. St. Mary's has its own distinctive qualities, it has its trademarks, which set it apart and which give it a specific character.

The first of these trademarks is the total and unreserved commitment to Catholic education which St. Mary's has had from the very beginning. It had no more than opened its doors in the original block building on 8th and White Streets when classes, in both sacred and secular subjects, were held in its basement rooms. Since that day, with a single brief interruption, St. Mary's has provided a sound basic elementary education for its children. One of its most outstanding accomplishments in the field of education was the founding of the memorable St. Mary's High School for Boys, staffed by Brothers of Mary; a school which flourished here for 22 years, and which has left an indelible imprint on this city.

Another distinguishing feature of this parish has been its profound sense of community. By its very structure, every parish is a community center; but at St. Mary's this function has been carried out with special emphasis. This congregation does not only pray together; it plays and works and rejoices together. In the 1880s and 1890s, St. Mary's became a hub of every field of activity — spiritual, athletic, and artistic. From the early 1900s, the halls of the famous Casino rang with the applause of theater audiences, with the cheers of sports fans, and with the strains of music, as parishioners and their friends came together to attend plays and games, to dance or to simply enjoy one another's company.

In carrying out this function as a community center, St. Mary's has shown an unusual sensitivity, responsiveness to the needs of her people. In the lean years of the Depression, when needs were more elemental, the hungry came to the rectory door in great numbers and none was ever turned away. Many a man in those days owed his life to the charity of the pastor, the housekeepers, and the parishioners who gave what little surplus they had to others. In those difficult days, wise heads knew that food provided but a temporary solution to their problems.

It is only when a man is willing to invest in the future that he gains some control over its direction. And so was born the St. Mary's Credit Union, soon to become the largest parish credit union in the state of Iowa. Long before the federal government sponsored the hot lunch program, St. Mary's served free meals to the children in her casino dining room. And today the Washington Opportunity Center and the Self-Help programs are the modern continuations of those earlier programs of social welfare. St. Mary's has truly been almost a city by itself.

A third feature that is distinctive of St. Mary's is difficult to put into words. I am thinking of the tradition of this parish to "go first class" in all things, and I might call this feature the commitment of St. Mary's to quality. This parish could hardly be called affluent; yet there is no evidence that it has ever given the slightest consideration to the second best, to the second rate, when either the worship of God or the education of her children was involved.

Liturgical art is the silent teacher of theology and the architecture of St. Mary's church, the epitome of Gothic style; its magnificent interior with its frescoed walls, its beautiful stations, windows and altars, all these are the rich source of knowledge and inspiration.

Education is the telescope of the mind and St. Mary's has spared no effort to give her children the very best, at the parish level and in its support of Wahlert High School.

Music is the color vehicle of prayer: scarcely had the parishioners moved into their new church, when they installed an organ whose equal was not to be found in the *entire Midwest. An instrument whose purchase brought the wondering exclamation from a man in the East: "an organ like this west of the Mississippi in 1870?" Had this man heard one of the great choirs of St. Mary's or had he listened to its congregation sing, his wonderment would have been less.*

There are other trademarks of St. Mary's but these seem to me to be pre-eminent: the commitment of St. Mary's to Catholic education, to community service, and to quality.

It is not easy to measure success, particularly in the spiritual realm. Yet I believe that these qualities would lead most men to consider St. Mary's as being eminently successful in carrying out its mandate to serve the People of God. Today we search for the cause of the success of St. Mary's and we find these causes to be many.

One of the most obvious reasons for the outstanding position which St. Mary's occupies today is her priests. Without in any way deprecating the wonderful assistants who have served St. Mary's through the years, I speak here especially of the pastors of this parish. As I read in the centennial booklet the litany of names of these former pastors, each name rings out with all the power and clarity of the great bells of this church. As I review their accomplishments, the passage of Genesis runs like a refrain through the mind: "Giants were upon the earth in those days." (Genesis 6:4) Giants were indeed there at St. Mary's yet none casts a longer shadow than does your present pastor. And when the history of this parish is rewritten by other hands, he will be reckoned a pastor among pastors; for even in the company of giants he has been found to have stature.

A second reason for the success of St. Mary's is the sisters who have faithfully served this parish for the past 98 years. Other congregations tarried here briefly, but the Franciscans have devoted three generations to St. Mary's Church, and to the children of this parish. Their brown habit, reflecting the earth of the Midwest, and signifying their fundamental humility and simplicity of life, has been a symbol in this parish of all that is good in Christianity.

Sometimes, I am sure, these sisters must wonder how effective is their educational work, and whether perhaps another form of apostolate might not bring greater returns. They would be reassured if they knew how their names are held in respect in so many thousands of homes, not only in Dubuque, but wherever Dubuquers have traveled.

During their recent fund drive, in which by the way St. Mary's has taken the lead, I visited a local business man; he asked me when someone was going to approach him because he wanted to give. He said, "Father, those sisters taught me in school; what they gave me I can never repay and I owe them more than anyone can imagine." Frankly, I believe that we have all been too reticent in telling the Sisters how grateful we are for their truly wonderful work.

The labor of the priests and the sisters of this parish has been of prime importance for its success and its growth. But no single contribution could be greater than the deep, abiding faith of its parishioners. Monsignor O'Malley once said of them: "they believe that Christ is God, and they show it in their lives." A faith that made light of all obstacles when this church was first planned; a faith that has carried this parish through every crises; a faith that has flowered and has given to the church almost 100 vocations, one for each year of its existence.

There is a final reason why this parish has enjoyed such unusual success. And this is its dedication to Mary, the Mother of God. Reverence for the Mother brings favors from the Son. This reverence goes beyond the simple act of naming the church after Mary and dedicating it to the mystery of her Assumption. It is to be found in a living and meaningful devotion to Mary, expressed here in so many ways.

St. Mary's Legion of Mary has flourished, for both men and women; twice weekly since 1938 there has been offered a novena to Mary under her title Mother of Perpetual Help. For many years, the Marian Day of Catholic Action Week was held annually in this church and the special devotion of the parishioners to Mary is reflected in a permanent way in the beautiful Marian altar of carrara marble which graces the sanctuary.

Today we join the members of this parish in thanking God and Mary for the shelter which this church as given; for the inspiration and the nourishment which it has occasioned, for a hundred years. Here, so many of you have been washed in the waters of baptism and have entered the family of Christians. Here, you have received strength to meet the obstacles of the adult world though anointing with Holy Chrism. When you sinned, it was here that you sought and obtained forgiveness. Here you have beheld the wondrous act of Christ becoming present, and have received His flesh and blood in the Eucharistic meal. Here your married life began with a sacramental outpouring of grace. And when your work is done, and you have breathed your last breath, it is this place that your remains will be brought to receive the final blessings.

We give thanks to God, then for His protection and His preservation of this church. We return thanks to Him for all the graces that He has showered upon his congregation. And since each generation must earn anew its own blessings, we humbly ask that we may continue to deserve the favor which God has shown this parish for a hundred years and more. —Father Friedl (1967)

Cross on Ceiling
Photo © 2009, Don Long, Jr.

28 October 1967

The Rev. Anthony W. Sigwarth
Saint Mary's Parish
1584 White Street
Dubuque, Iowa

Dear Father Sigwarth,

We "thank God today in jubilation" as you and your people of "beloved St. Mary's" celebrate one hundred years of the "new" church so filled with old memories.

You, Father, who have dedicated the younger and middle years of your priesthood to the people, especially the poor, within St. Mary's boundaries — you must be exultant today.

We are certain that our Sisters in heaven who gave so much of their lives to St. Mary's are rejoicing, too. The occasion is a special happiness to those Sisters who are "girls from St. Mary's."

You have an interesting and valuable Centennial Brochure, Father, one that must have taken months in the making. Thank you for the invitation, the brochure and the book of verse.

And congratulations on your appointment as Dean of Dubuque. May St. Mary's be a leader in renewal!

    Sincerely in Christ,

    Mother Mary Matilda and
    The Sisters of Mount St. Francis

One year, the police got a tip that someone overheard a conversation about a plan to rob Msgr. Anthony Sigwarth when he returned from his annual Sunday night trip to Bingo to bring the loot back to the rectory in his famous black bag. So one of the policemen, about his size, was going to be a decoy. He practiced walking like Msgr. and put on his black hat and coat and carried the black bag. We sisters watched from the music room window as he shuffled out of the rectory and across 16th Street to Sigwarth Hall and later came back. But there was no excitement. The would be robbers must have known about the plan and no one attempted to rob the "decoy."
—Sr. Carol Hoverman (2010)

[Sr. Carol Hoverman was a music teacher at St. Mary's School. She is currently the editor of *The Witness*]

Reverend Sigwarth served as pastor until 1977. He passed away December 27, 1985; his funeral was at his beloved St. Mary's.

1977 — Present

Reverend Richard Krapfl served as pastor from 1977 through 1982. He currently is on special assignment in the Archdiocese.

Reverend Paul Steimel born in Waterloo, Iowa, was ordained on June 7, 1952. He served as pastor from 1982 through 1993. He next served at St. Patrick's Church in Cedar Falls, Iowa, until he retired in 1997.

Reverend Florian Schmidt was born in Springbrook, Iowa. He was ordained on March 18, 1961. He came to pastor the members of St. Mary's in 1993 and he served until 1999. He was awarded the Dean of Ossian Deanery in 1984. Reverend Schmidt retired in 2002.

Ardel Henry Barta was born in Fairfax, Iowa. He attended Loras College in Dubuque and Mount Saint Bernard Seminary in Dubuque. He was ordained on March 9, 1963, by Bishop George Biskup at Cedar Rapids, Iowa.

Funeral of Reverend Sigwarth
Contributed by St. Mary Church Archives

Close up of Angel on Ceiling
Photo © 2009, Don Long, Jr.

Father Barta was assigned to St. Patrick's Church in Dubuque in July 1997, as Sacramental Priest and the Associate Master of Ceremonies to the Archbishop. In 1999, his assignment was extended to include St. Mary's Church.

In 1999, St. Mary's and St. Patrick's churches were clustered, retaining their own identities but sharing administration and priests due to the shortage in available priests. Deacon Tim LoBianco was appointed Pastoral Administrator of both parishes. (Bowerman, 2004)

> *When Deacon Tim [LoBianco] first asked me to be the secretary here I said no. I had NO experience as a secretary. I couldn't type or fuss with the computer for sure. He didn't care, he wanted to hire me for my "front door ministry." He felt my personality was what was needed here and the rest would come. I prayed a lot and finally said yes.*
>
> *We started together on July 13, 1999. For the first month I spent most of the time straightening up the files in the closet under the stairs. This room was called the 'bootsie' room, so whenever Tim would come down to St. Mary's he would find me in the "bootsie" room. My nickname became Bootsie.*
>
> *I rapidly came to learn the runnings of a parish. My front door ministry was easy, until one day I answered the door and a man came in and knelt down in the entry way. He was insistent that I hear his confession and he wouldn't get up until I did. I repeatedly and gently refused trying to get him to understand but to no avail. I finally put my hand on his head and said, "May the Peace of Christ be with you," and he got up and went away.*
>
> *I have always tried my best to welcome and treat everyone at the door as if they were Christ Himself asking for help. I can only hope I have succeeded in a small way, accepting people as they are.* —Jackie Williams, Secretary (2010)

Reverend Richard Krapfl
Pastor (1977–1982)

Reverend Paul Steimel
Pastor (1982–1993)

Photos contributed by Archdiocese of Dubuque Archives

Last Pastor

Father Steven Rosonke took over as pastor in July of 2008, when Father Ardel Barta retired. Father Rosonke was ordained on May 29, 1982. Prior to serving St. Mary's and St. Patrick's, he had been assigned to St. Patrick's Church in Cedar Rapids, Iowa.

During his tenure in Cedar Rapids (1996–2008), he assisted many who lived in the parish district. His reassignment to Dubuque followed on the heels of the flood of 2008 where Father Rosonke served the needs of flood victims.

> *Father Steve Rosonke, current pastor of St. Patrick's and St. Mary's, one time incorporated the daily scripture reading and St. Mary's altar into his homily. Father mentioned that St. Mary's altar was made of hundreds of pieces that created a beautiful mosaic altar. The same way the Church is made up of many people to create one church.* —Dave Becker (2010)

Reverend Florian J. Schmidt, Pastor (1993–1999)
Contributed by Dubuque Archdiocese Archives

Reverend Krapfl with First Communicant, Candice (Kelley) Chaloupka
Contributed by Candice Chaloupka

Reverend Steven J. Rosonke, Pastor (2008–2010)
Contributed by Dubuque Archdiocese Archives

Father Ardel Barta, Pastor (1999–2008)
Contributed by St. Mary's Church Archives

Thank you, Jackie, Annie, and Father Steve for your years of faithful service to the members of St. Mary's Parish. Your kindness, love, support and dedication will not be forgotten.

May the Lord Bless you and keep you!
May the Lord let his face shine upon you, and be gracious to you!
May the Lord look upon you kindly and give you peace!
—Numbers 6:24-26 (NAB)

Jackie Williams, Secretary; Father Steve Rosonke;
and Annie Wertz, Pastoral Associate (2009)
Contributed by St. Mary Church Archives

Sacristy
Photo © 2009, Candice Chaloupka

Altar
Photo © 2009, Candice Chaloupka

Inside St. Mary's

The interior of St. Mary's has seen many changes over it's history. The first renovations started soon after it was built and more funding became available. Often the changes were made to accommodate ever-growing congregations and to repair damages caused by the ravages of time.

Organ

In 1870, the parish commissioned the E. and G. G. Hook Company of Boston to build a three manual tracker-action organ with thirty–three registers and twenty–six speaking stops. They paid $6,000 for it. At the time it was installed, it was the largest organ in the state. Many renowned musicians considered it a masterful instrument "with exceptional tonal qualities." Even now, to see another one like it, one would have to go to Yale University.

It was rebuilt in 1965 by Earl Beilharz of the Lima Organ Company out of Alida, OH. The original 1,500 pipes were repaired, three new stops were added, and the action was changed to an electric. A new console, blower, and chests were also installed. (Sigwarth, 1967)

My wife and I joined St. Mary's Parish in 1996. My wife is multi-talented. Unfortunately, I am not. I have one hobby and that is playing organ. And in October 2007, I auditioned for an organist position at St. Mary's that would open in November. I had practiced on the Hook & Hastings [the E. & G.G. Hook company became the Hook & Hastings in 1872] organ at St. Mary's for a couple of hours the week before I was supposed to start my weekly service. Everything seemed fine.

The first Sunday I played was November 18, 2007. As I climbed the steps and unlocked the door to the choir loft, and sat down at the organ, something wonderful happened. I noticed that from the organ bench I was in line with the Cross on the top of the wooden Altar. Since the organist sits with his or her back to the front of the church, there are two mirrors to assist the organist. I started taking in the beautiful paintings and the stained glass windows throughout the church.

I knew that I was part of something very special. I was somewhat overcome with emotion. I wish that everyone could see the rare beauty of St. Mary's from the organ loft. You are taught to look down when praying. In St. Mary's you should look up!! How many have seen the Sanctus, Sanctus, Sanctus, in the arch over the Altar?

Well, the Mass started and the music swelled. That was 2 ½ years ago. They say that because of the practicing involved, that playing an organ is a labor of love. I agree!

One Sunday, Monsignor David Wheeler was saying Mass. We started a different Mass setting that week and I practiced the music for several hours. As with all performing musicians, occasionally mistakes happen. Well, when I played the Holy, Holy, Holy, I got one finger out of place and made a couple of mistakes. I went up to talk

with Monsignor Wheeler. Before I could say anything, he said to me "You are concerned about the little mistake you made." I said "Yes!" The Monsignor said that many people did not even notice it. He then said something that caught me totally off guard. With graciousness and caring, the Monsignor said that he was in awe of me!!! Me, a boy from the little town of Sherrill, Iowa. He then asked "How many notes were you playing at the time of the mistakes?" I said 7 on 2 different keyboards plus one by foot. He mentioned that he played the trumpet and that he only had to worry about 1 note at a time and that was enough for him. The Monsignor continued "how you people [organists] can put together numerous notes on different keyboards, play the pedal board with our feet, and manage the voices, volume and couplers of the organ is truly a God-given talent."
I agreed!

I will always cherish the truly unique and very special position as one of St. Mary's organists. My wife and I are happy to have been a part of the St. Mary's family.
—Russell Nauman (2010)

Ceiling Fresco Close up
Photo © 2009, Don Long, Jr.

Telegraph Herald

July 30, 2009

Saturday Concert will showcase St. Mary's Organ

Sister Mary Arnold Staudt, assistant professor of music at Briar Cliff University in Sioux City, Iowa, will play a concert showcasing the historic pipe organ at St. Mary's Church, 15th and White streets in Dubuque, at 3 p.m. Saturday, August 1, preceding the 4 p.m. Mass.

In the records of the Hook Organ Company of Boston, in 1870, appeared the following entry according to E.A. Broadway, historian of the organ company: "A Three Manual Tracker-Action Organ, Thirty-three registers, twenty-six speaking stops. An organ like this west of the Mississippi in 1870?"

The organ was rebuilt and electrified in 1965.

© 2009 Telegraph Herald. Reprinted with permission.

Hook Organ
Photo © 2009, Don Long, Jr.

Hook Organ
Photo © 2009, Don Long, Jr.

Hook Organ
Photo © 2009, Candice Chaloupka

Bells

Adding to the musical worship experience at St. Mary's were the three bells installed in the steeple tower in 1876, 1878, and 1883. The largest bell weighed 5,000 lbs. Cast by the Stuckstede Brothers Bell Foundry of St. Louis, Missouri, they were dedicated to St. John the Apostle, the Blessed Virgin, and the Crucifixion.

Automatic bell ringing equipment was installed in 1946 by parishioner William Klauer. He paid $3,000. Through May 2010 they could be heard at noon and 6 p.m. (St. Mary's Church Archives, 1962)

Renovations

Over the course of 1911 through 1914, a campaign for capital expenditures was conducted and about $40,000 was spent on renovating and enlarging the church.

In 1912, four side entrances were added to the church along with confessional chapels. The sanctuary was enlarged and the roof was redone with slate. A stucco coating was also applied to the brick facade. Other enhancements to the interior included paintings of the Stations of the Cross, stained glass windows, and statues from Munich, Bavaria.

Outside of Chapel
Photo © 2010, Candice Chaloupka

The Pieta
Photo © 2009, Don Long, Jr.

Agony in the Garden
Photo © 2009, Candice Chaloupka

Bricked-in Rose Window
Photo © 2009, Candice Chaloupka

Mural

In 1912, the Brielmaier family from Milwaukee, Wisconsin, was commissioned to draw up and paint frescoes. A mural was also commissioned to be painted behind the altar to replace the rose window. This rose window can be seen from outside the church, though the circle has been bricked in.

Sadly, the elder Brielmaier died before the work was completed so the paintings, excepting the mural, were sublet to the Joseph Walter Company, church decorators in Dubuque. The church paid $4,078.50 for the frescoes.

Matilda (also listed as Lottie) Brielmaier was commissioned to paint a large fresco on the wall behind the altar. Since St. Mary's was under the patronage of our Blessed Mother's Assumption, she felt this should be the theme of the mural.

> *The story ascribed to the mural is that when Mary died and was assumed into heaven, all the apostles were there, except Thomas. When the other apostles told him he said "Show me." They took him to the tomb and opened it. It was full of roses and lilies. Above Thomas' head is Mary. She has dropped her sash and it is around his neck. Above*

> *Mary is the Trinity, ready to crown her Queen of Heaven.*
> (Brochure, 2007)

Matilda began painting the mural in her studio in Milwaukee on three canvases. She finished painting it when the canvases were mounted on the wall in the church. She wanted the mural to be large enough that "eyes are drawn to it as one enters the church." (Brochure, 2007) Matilda also painted many of the other large pictures in the church.

Due to the "constant and extreme changes of temperature" the canvas was shriveled and the colors and figures had all but disappeared. To address this, in 1943, Carl Stringham, an artist from St. Louis, restored the fading and curling mural. His murals and paintings were found in many churches throughout the country.

> *Mr. Stringham admirably succeeded in restoring not only the work of Miss Brielmaier, but has given us a new Virgin after the famous paint of Murillo. Thus the whole picture is based upon a story concerning the Assumption embodied in the well known paint of Andrea del Sarto.* (Zeyen, 1943)

The mural was restored again in 1955.

> *Behind the main altar at St. Mary's on the ceiling is a beautiful Mural of the Assumption of Mary. Instead of a halo around the Saints heads, one the saints has a triangle around his head. That triangle represents the Holy Trinity. I have never seen a triangle around a Saint in all the churches that I have visited. They all have Halos around their head.* —Dave Becker (2010)

Assumption Mural
Photo © 2009, Candice Chaloupka

The Stations of the Cross

The Stations of the Cross paintings were also commissioned and installed around 1912, along with the stained glass windows of Mary and other statuary. All of these beautiful works of art came from Munich, Bavaria.

Originally the text printed under the Stations was written in German but with the rise in anti-German sentiment as a result of World War II, the text was changed to English.

Inside St. Mary's

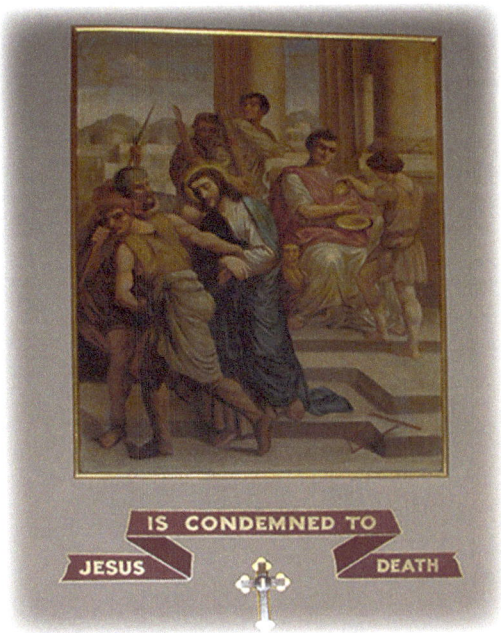

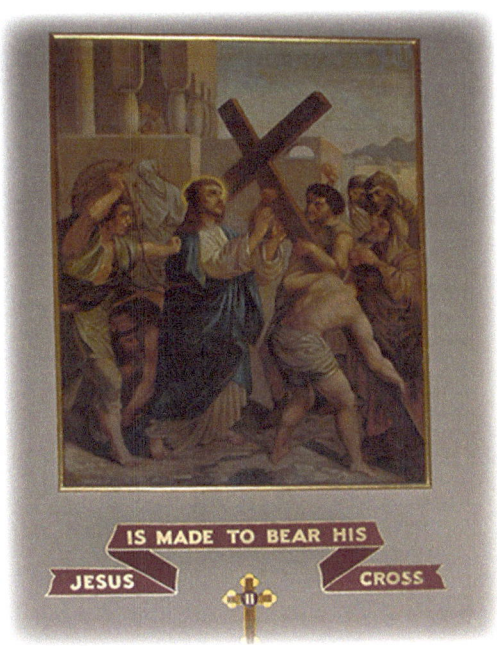

Stations of the Cross
Photos © 2010, Barb Ehlers

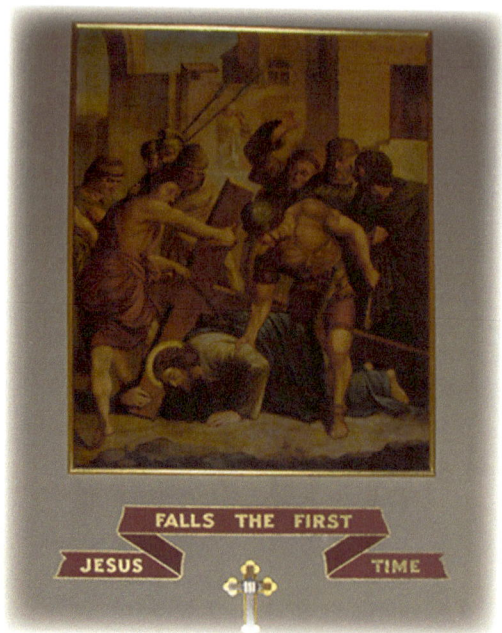

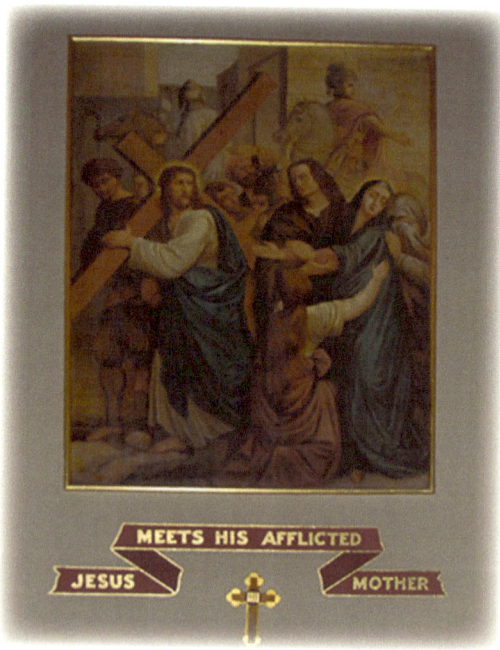

Stations of the Cross
Photos © 2010, Barb Ehlers

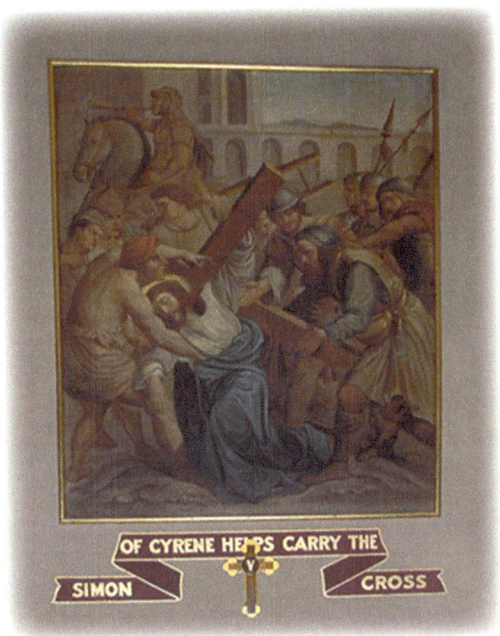

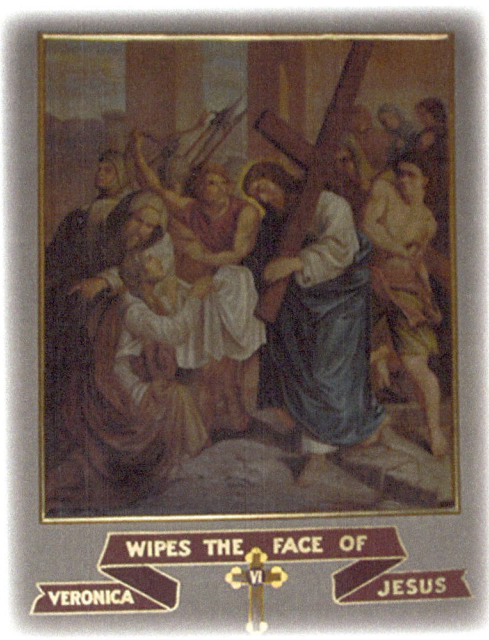

Stations of the Cross
Photos © 2010, Barb Ehlers

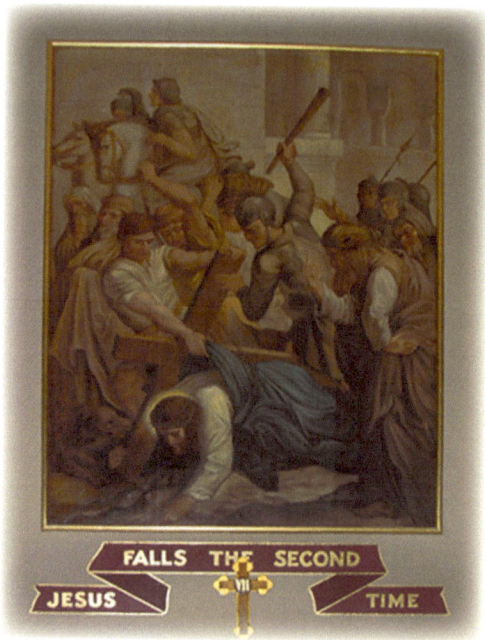

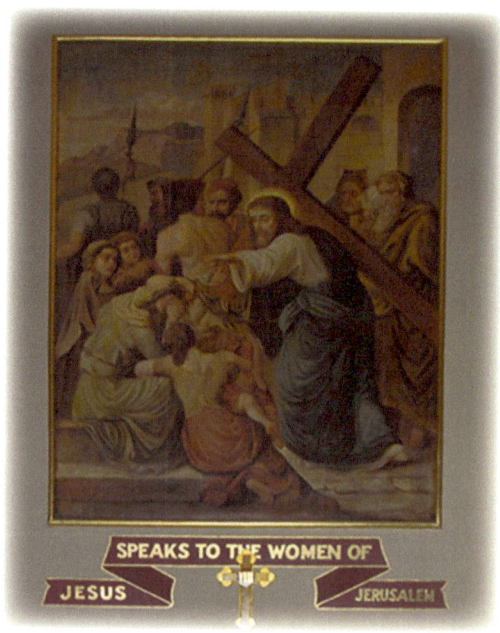

Stations of the Cross
Photos © 2010, Barb Ehlers

Inside St. Mary's

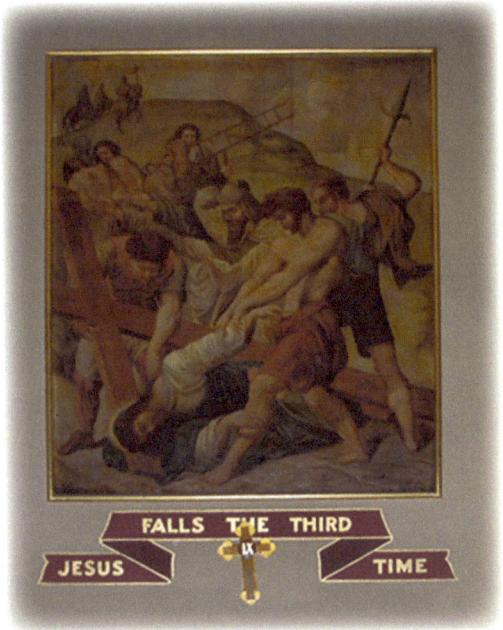

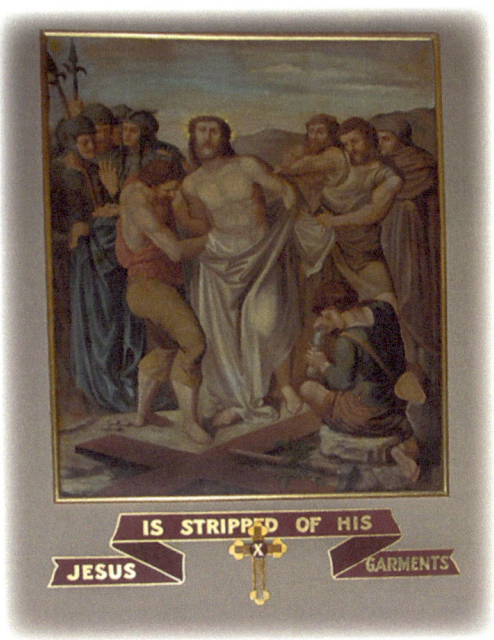

Stations of the Cross
Photos © 2010, Barb Ehlers

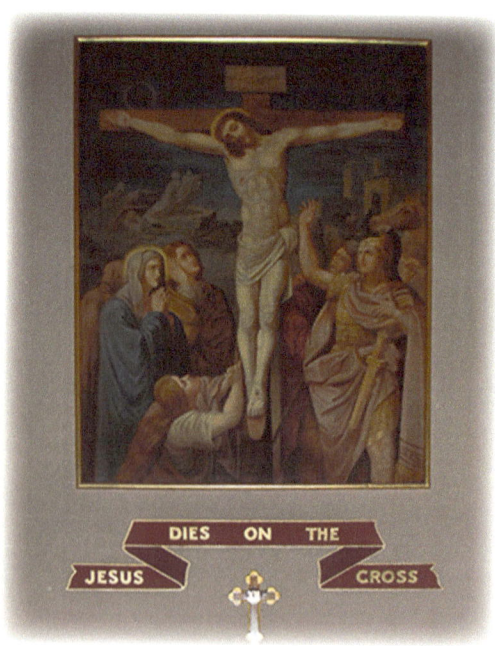

Stations of the Cross
Photos © 2010, Barb Ehlers

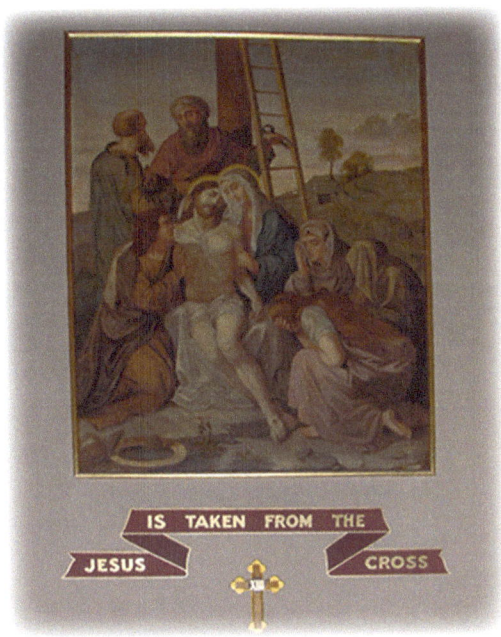

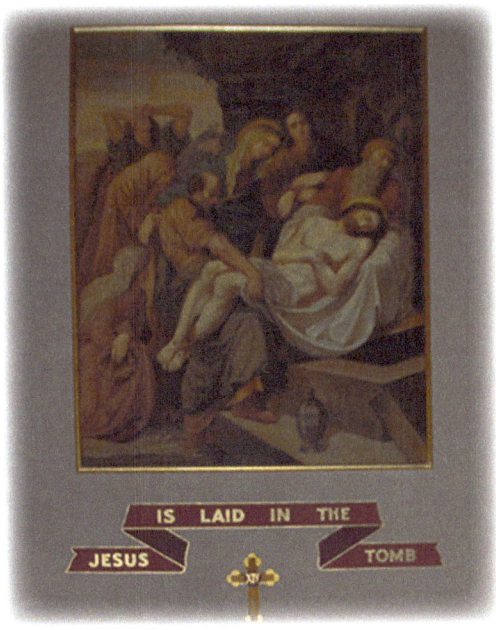

Stations of the Cross
Photos © 2010, Barb Ehlers

Stained Glass in Sacristy
Photo © 2010, Don Long, Jr.

Stained Glass Windows

During the early period of the church, congregations were largely illiterate. So the early church used stained glass windows to communicate Bible stories. St. Mary's Church has many beautiful stained glass windows in addition to the twelve that were commissioned to depict the life of Mary from her presentation in the temple to the scene of her death.

The stained glass windows were purchased from the Zetteler Company for $700.00 each. The artist, F.X. Zetteler, was considered a master artist and was held in high regard.

> Both the Mayer and Zettler Studios perfected what became known as the "Munich Style," which was copied by more than a dozen other window makers who set up shop in

the area. The new style allowed for extremely detailed depictions of their subjects. The scenes depicted were heavily influenced by the emotion and sentimentality of the 19th century European Romantic style of painting, and the detail and ornateness of the German Baroque style.

Zettler is widely recognized as the master of perspective (where an object in the background of a scene is depicted as smaller than the object in the foreground, giving a sense of depth). He is also is credited with being the first to use three-point perspective in stained glass windows. Zettler's scenes looked more like the landscaped paintings of the Renaissance and after.

The Munich Style and three-point perspective were later adapted and modified by the great American designer, Louis Comfort Tiffany. While the latter's name may be more known to people today, in their own era it was apparent who was the master and who was the student: at the 1893 World's Columbian Exposition in Chicago, a Zettler window won top prize over a Tiffany! (http://louisville-catholic.net)

There was concern that the impending conflict in Germany might impede shipment of the windows. Fortunately, they were able to complete the windows and they were shipped before war broke out in Germany. (Sigwarth, 1967)

St. Mary's in Dubuque was fortunate to receive their windows when they did:

Holy Rosary Church in Cedar, Michigan, ordered windows from Zettler just before the outbreak of World War I. The firm made the windows, but the war erupted before they could be shipped. Zettler's firm buried the windows in Germany to keep them from being damaged, and then sent them to the U.S. after the conflict ended.

St. Mary Magdalen in Camarillo, California, purchased windows in 1913, but did not receive them due to the war. It was believed that they had been part of a shipment on a freighter which had been destroyed in the Atlantic while en route to America. In 1919, the windows were discovered safely packed away in crates in Germany, and were then forwarded to their California owners.
(http://louisville-catholic.net)

Archangels, Stained Glass in Chapels
Photos © 2009, Candice Chaloupka

Archangels, Stained Glass in Chapels
Photos © 2009, Candice Chaloupka

Archangels, Stained Glass in Chapels
Photos © 2009, Candice Chaloupka

Archangels, Stained Glass in Chapels
Photos © 2009, Candice Chaloupka

Stained Glass in Choir Loft
Photo © 2009, Don Long, Jr.

Stained Glass in Choir Loft
Photo © 2009, Don Long, Jr.

Stained Glass in Choir Loft
Photo © 2009, Don Long, Jr.

Mary's story unfolds in the procession of stained glass windows beginning on the west side of the Sanctuary.

**Presentation of
the Blessed Virgin Mary**
Mary's childhood is not told of in the scriptures but is revealed to us through Sacred Tradition. Here we see Mary being presented at the temple into the service of God.

**Annunciation of
the Blessed Virgin Mary**
Hail Mary Full of Grace, the Lord is with you!...The Holy Spirit will come upon you...Therefore the child to be born will be called, holy, the Son of God...Mary said...May it be done to me according to your word.
Luke 1:28–38

Photos © 2010, Barb Ehlers

Engagement of Joseph and Mary

The angel of the Lord appeared to Joseph in a dream and said, Joseph, do not be afraid to take Mary your wife into your home…When Joseph awoke, he did as the angel of the Lord commanded him. Matthew 1:20–24

Visitation of Mary to Elizabeth
When Mary her relative Elizabeth was also going to have a baby she went to see her. When Elizabeth heard Mary's voice, she cried out, "Most blessed are you among women and blessed is the fruit of your womb!" Luke 1:39–45

Photos © 2010, Barb Ehlers

The Epiphany
Behold, Magi from the east arrived in Jerusalem, saying "Where is the newborn king of the Jews?" And on entering the house they saw the child with Mary his other…and did him homage. Matthew 2:2–12

Presentation of Child Jesus in the Temple
They took him up to Jerusalem to present him to the Lord. Luke 2:22

Photos © 2010, Barb Ehlers

The Flight into Egypt

The angel of the Lord appeared to Joseph in a dream and said, "rise, take the child and his mother, flee to Egypt, and stay there until I tell you." Matthew 2:13

Finding of Child Jesus in the Temple

After three days they found him in the temple, sitting in the midst of the teachers, listening to them, asking them questions, all who heard him were astounded. Luke 2:46–47

Photos © 2010, Barb Ehlers

The Holy Family at Nazareth
He went down with them and came to Nazareth, and was obedient to them. Luke 2:51

Wedding Feast at Cana
Jesus told them, "Fill the jars with water… Then he told them, draw some out now and take it to the headwaiter…And when the headwaiter tasted the water that had become wine. John 2:7–9

Photos © 2010, Barb Ehlers

Inside St. Mary's

Jesus Appears to Mary after His Resurrection

The angel said to the women, "He is not here, for he has been raised just as he said." And behold, Jesus met them on their way and greeted them. Mathew 28: 5–6, 9

The Death of Mary

According to Sacred Tradition, Mary lived 72 years on earth. Here she is depicted surrounded by other faithful followers of Jesus.

Photos © 2010, Barb Ehlers

Altar of St. Mary

Altar of St. Mary
Photo © 2009, Candice Chaloupka

The Altar of St. Mary was installed in 1928. This beautiful altar in Mary's honor was crafted of Italian Carrara marble. The mosaic, "Mary of the Angels" was imported from Munich, Bavaria.

Mosaic in Altar of St. Mary
Photo © 2009, Candice Chaloupka

Relics in Altar of St. Mary
Photo © 2009, Candice Chaloupka

Relics

Contained within the altar are relics from St. Francis, St. Anthony, St. Clement Hofbauer, and St. Peter Canisius. Relics of Saints help to recall to mind the example of a particular saint.

> *St. Francis of Assisi* — Patron saint of animals and ecology. He took the gospel literally, following all Jesus said and did. Several religious and secular orders were founded as a response to his biblical teachings.
>
> *St. Anthony of Padua* — Patron saint of lost and stolen articles. He was a Franciscan preacher and teacher.
>
> *St. Clement Hofbauer* — Apostle and Patron to Vienna. He devoted himself to glorifying God and drawing others to serve him. Saint Clement is a model for all people.
>
> *St. Peter Canisius* — Patron of Germany. An important figure in the Catholic Reformation in Germany. He is regarded as one of the creators of the Catholic Press.

Our Lady of Perpetual Help

Our Lady of Perpetual Help
Photo © 2009, Candice Chaloupka

Our Lady of Perpetual Help is an icon: a picture that tells a story. It is not known who the artist was, but it is believed it was painted sometime in the 13th century. Mary's image is somber and she looks to the viewer, not her son. Jesus is portrayed clinging to his mother, seeking comfort, and has a sandal dangling from his foot.

Along with the image of the Blessed Virgin with Jesus, the left side of the icon depicts the Archangel Michael carrying the lance and sponge from the crucifixion of Jesus. The right side depicts the Archangel Gabriel carrying a three-bar cross and nails.

The Greek initials above Mary and Jesus read "Mother of God, Michael Archangel, Gabriel Archangel, and Jesus Christ. The painting holds the message: "You can come to me."

The shrine to Our Lady of Perpetual Help was erected in 1938. A Novena was said from March 27 through April 5, 1938, by Rev. Joseph Printon and two novenas were conducted weekly on Tuesdays for a number of years. The average attendance at the Novena to Our Lady of Perpetual Help, held every Tuesday morning and evening, was at least 1,500 per week.

Shrine to Our Lady of Perpetual Help
Photo © 2009, Candice Chaloupka

1954 — The Year of Mary

In 1954, Pope Pius XII designated 1954 as the "Year of Mary". Many people made pilgrimages to St. Mary's Church during the Marian year with 28,000 Marian leaflets distributed to the many visitors.

Since Ash Wednesday that year and throughout the year, it was rare not to find some five to ten people in the church making visits throughout the day. This continued up to eight o' clock in the evening and on Sundays and Holy Days even later. There was a real noticeable increase in daily communions, especially among the children. There were many more than usual who also took advantage of the numerous opportunities to receive the sacrament of Penance.

There were at least two pilgrimages per week from the Solemn Pontifical on April 3rd by Archbishop Binz up to the closing date. In addition to the Dubuque parishes — societies from the Dominican Priory, Key West, St. Joseph's, Holy Cross, Luxenburg, Richardsville, New Vienna, Dyersville, Sherrill, St. Catherine's, Galena, East Dubuque, Ill: Hanover, Ill; and Darlington, Cuba City, Shullsburg, Dickeyville, Cassville, and Potosi, Wisconsin, had various and many pilgrimages. The students from the Academies and Loras and Clarke Colleges made repeated pilgrimages to the Church.

The Marian Year Prayer was added to all devotions; the regular Sunday and Novena devotions and the special ones during Lent.

Renovations

In 1957, it was decided the church needed redecorating. Twice during the prior 40 years the walls had been repainted and mosaics renewed but a complete renovation needed to be done.

Although it was agreed that it would have been cheaper and easier to modernize, St. Mary's was an historical landmark and parishioners felt the masterpieces should be reproduced. So in three installments, the John C. Kaiser Company of Dubuque began renovations, first to the sanctuary, then the side walls, and finally the nave.

Such care and diligence was used that the chief artist, John Strelesky, used a one–hair brush on the eyes of the angels. The talented artist crafted images that are so extraordinary that the character's garments seem to move in the murals.

Although the main altar's gold-leafing was not in the contract for renovation, Monsignor Klott paid for and helped to regild the gold-leafing on the main altar. Jim and John Fabricius also helped by volunteering every night after work for nine months. (Mary Ann Fabricius, email message to author, May 27, 2010)

> *The church finance committee was going to paint the gold altar but Monsignor Klott fought it and regilded it himself.*
> —Sister Mary Ann Wagner (2010)

Angel
Photo © 2009, Don Long, Jr.

Angels
Photo © 2009, Don Long, Jr.

The 1960s was a period of great generosity on the part of the parishioners for maintenance of the other parish buildings. In 1961, the stucco coating applied in 1912 was removed and the original brick was weather-proofed, tuck-pointed, and painted. This cost an additional $26,000.

The rectory was tuck-pointed in 1962 and the lots on the southwest corner of 15th and White Streets were donated by Miss Regina Walter and used for parking.

1962 also saw the addition of new light fixtures and the tower clock at a cost of $2,280, given by an anonymous donor who also donated the electrically lit Gloria in Excelsis Deo banner that was put above the nativity display. Sadly, this banner was destroyed in the 1976 fire.

High Altar
Photos © 2009, Candice Chaloupka

High Altar
Photos © 2009, Don Long, Jr.

The year 1965 brought a new entry for the church and carpet, donated by an anonymous parishioner.

The Klauer foundation donated the new vinyl floor for under the pews which were refurnished and another donor supplied new carpet. Also that year, an anonymous donor provided funds to illuminate the tower of the church. The mosaics were also framed.

For the 1967 centennial celebration, the Greco Artists of Chicago donated and installed the bronze doors which are decorated with the fleur de lis emblems. Another source stated the cost at $32,000 for the 12 doors. (1976 history)

The steeple was repainted in 1968 along with the window frames. The 16–foot cross on the steeple was also gold-leafed, costing $9,368.70. A new church roof was installed in 1975 at a cost of $94,760.00.

Vatican II Changes

The First Sunday of Advent 1964, was the first Mass was said in the English vernacular with the congregation participating. Other changes soon followed: the communion rail was removed in 1966 and a new altar that faced the congregation was placed in the sanctuary. The original high and side altars were left largely intact.

Nativity with Donated Gloria in Excelsis Deo Banner
Contributed by St. Mary's Church Archives

Before the changes instituted by Vatican II, people often prayed the rosary during the mass, they attended but did not participate. It was like watching a movie, but it was always the same movie. Mass is so much more now.
—Sister Marie Therese Kalb (2010)

St. Mary's with Communion Rail
Photo contributed by St. Mary's Church Archives

Fleur de Lis on Bronze Doors
Photo © 2010, Candice Chaloupka

Fire of 1976

On January 9, 1976, a fire started next to the Nativity scene in front of the altar of St. Joseph.

> *Way back in the twenties the church wiring had been put into conduit, but at a turn in the basement, through vibration from heavy traffic and from lightning bolts that at times had jumped from lightening rod cables to the conduit, at a break in the conduit a "short" developed and fire started smoldering up inside a wall, burnt plaster laths, and as oxygen hit the fire, it burst into flames in close proximity to the crib. When the trees surrounding the crib exploded in flames, the smoke filled the church and began to escape through the tower.* (St. Mary's History, 1976)

Telegraph Herald Article dated January 13, 1976
Contributed by Joy (Thurston) Oberhausen

People were alerted to the fire when smoke escaped above the pipes of the organ and out the steeple. The fire department responded quickly and the church sustained minimal damage. The fire was hot enough though to melt light fixtures. The amplification system, chairs, and kneelers in the sanctuary were destroyed.

The figures from the nativity scene had been purchased from Munich; they were completely destroyed along with the crucifix. A stained glass window was sent to Chicago to be fixed; structural work was needed along with new carpet. The damages totaled $221,000. Fortunately, the Archdiocese had insurance to cover the damage.

The following Monday, over 200 volunteers arrived to help with the clean up and the John C. Kaiser Company, who refrescoed the church in 1956–57, began again to renovate. The gnarled light fixtures were sent back to the factory to be fixed. The organ had to be completely cleaned of soot and smoke, and parts were replaced.

Frescoed Ceiling
Photo © 2009, Don Long, Jr.

Crucifix Prior to 1976 Fire
Contributed by St. Mary's Church Archives

Replacement Crucifix Presently Hanging in Church
Photo © 2009, Don Long, Jr.

Light Fixture
Photo © 2009, Don Long, Jr.

This [fire] was nearly in the sanctuary. True, none of the church was burned up; but the entire ceiling was coated with smudge from the fire. Luckily, when a Dubuque company was hired to clean the ceiling, the beautiful designs were not harmed. There is a pillar on the right side, near the sanctuary. A series of Christmas lights were plugged into the outlet at the base of the pillar. That is where the fire started. I was there that night. One of the sisters from the convent called me down and told me that the pastor was so distraught that he might have a heart attack. She asked me to get him out of the church and back to the house, which I did. —Msgr. Friedl (2010)

 When I started [teaching] in August of 1976, there was still scaffolding up because they were still making repairs. The gold leafing around the altar was being worked on. I don't remember when it was completed.
—Sr. Josephine Schmitz (2010)

I worked at City Hall and was walking toward Ninth and Main Streets. I heard sirens and noticed black smoke bellowing upwards in the sky. Shortly afterwards I returned, following the smoke filled sky to St. Mary's Church. It was devastating to see the black smoke bellowing from the church steeple. The following day, I was able to see inside our beautiful church. The heat from the Christmas crib fire melted the ceiling light shades on the right side of the church; the black smoke painted the entire church with a film of black. It was unbelievable.

Fortunately, St. Mary's Church was restored to the beautiful church, as it is today; the most beautiful church in the Dubuque area. —Al Heitzman (2010)

Back in January of 1976, I lived two blocks from St. Mary's. I had just returned home from work on a January afternoon and saw smoke coming from St. Mary's Church. Luckily the firefighters controlled the amount of damage that was done to the church. The restoration job after the fire was done beautifully. —Dave Becker (2010)

In the 1990s, St. Mary's built a new handicapped entrance. This entrance is located at the northeast corner of the church, and has an elevator. Before that, the church was not as accessible as other churches in the area.

Six years ago I started being an altar server at St. Mary's for Funeral Masses. Being up on St. Mary's altar and looking out towards the murals, stained glass windows and the balcony made me see and appreciate the true beauty of St. Mary's. —Dave Becker (2010)

Angels on High
Photo © 2009, Don Long, Jr.

Frescoed Ceiling
Photo © 2009, Don Long, Jr.

Jackson Street School
Contributed by St. Mary's Church Archives

St. Mary's School

One of the most important ministries of the St. Mary's Parish was its role as educator to the parish's young. The first school opened in 1849. Classes were initially held in the basement of the old rock church.

Though the church did not have a permanent pastor, the families hired lay people to teach their children. The Sisters of Charity of the Blessed Virgin Mary took over the education after lay teachers had been dismissed by Father Emonds. They served until the Franciscans of Perpetual Adoration from La Crosse, Wisconsin, took over in 1869.

As the congregation grew, so did the school, although attendance ebbed from time to time due to economic concerns and political upheavals. The school closed for three years due to a financial crisis known as the "Panic of 1857." The Panic of 1857 began a period of severe economic depression that lasted three years in the United States. Many people lost their jobs, banks collapsed, and immigration to the United States, and Dubuque, Iowa, slowed and virtually stopped. (www.americaslibrary.com)

These sisters taught in the old rock church until they moved into the new convent in 1870. The convent served initially both as a home for the sisters and a classroom until the school was completed in 1872 (referred to as Jackson Street School). Sister Mary Ottilia Lutz, Sister Mary Gabriella Stricher, Sister Mary Theda Stoffer, and Sister Mary Stanislaus Huennekens were the first teachers. Two lay teachers, Miss Yungst and Januarius Higi (who was also organist), assisted the sisters in the care of more than two hundred pupils.

The teaching order changed for a third and final time in 1879 when the Sisters of St. Francis of the Holy Family were brought to Dubuque by Father Johannes. The sisters had come at the invitation of Bishop Hennessy. These sisters of the "brown habit" had been exiled from Germany under Bismarck and initially set up a shelter in Iowa City.

Their sole source of income had been an orphanage but the teaching assignment in Dubuque aided in their support. After a decade of service, the La Crosse sisters left reluctantly, but willingly, to make room for these new sisters from a different order.

> *The old church was meant to be only a temporary home, until the orphanage which the Bishop had invited the sisters to establish could be built. But the weeks turned into months, and there was precious little space for the sisters, the nine orphans they brought from Iowa City, and the postulants who were already entering the community in Dubuque. (Sisters of St. Francis Archives)*

Since St. Mary's was a German parish parents desired that classes be taught primarily in German — a perfect fit for the pioneer sisters! Sr. Bernarda Gelhaus and two postulants, who were American born, taught the English classes as were deemed necessary.

Sometime after 1879, the old stone building that had served as church and school was sold. It was used as a business until the 1960s when it was torn down. A memorial plaque is now where the old church once stood. (Hoffmann, 1938)

Dubuque Daily Herald

June 1, 1869   Page 3

A Pleasant Picnic

The annual picnic of the school connected with St. Mary's church took place yesterday at the Tivoll [spelling unclear in copy] Gardens, and a pleasant time it was for both old and young. At seven o'clock in the morning a large number met at the church and proceed from thence to Trinity church where the procession was organized. The Young Men's Association, the Pius Verein, the Alphonsus Verein, the School Verein and a large number of German citizens and children formed into procession, Andrew Heinzmann being marshal and Charles F. Thill assistant marshal.

From Trinity church the procession marched with two bands of music, up Seventh Street to Main and up that street to the gardens. Here the day was given over to pleasure and a happy time was had. What with two bands of music, lemonade, ice cream, strawberries, cakes and etc., a pleasant day and a cool breeze, if all did not enjoy themselves it was their own fault. A very large number was in attendance, including at least four hundred and fifty or five hundred members of St. Mary's German and English school. The proceeds must have been large and are devoted to the benefit of the school.

At noon the City Band proceeded to the residence of Mayor Knight to give him a serenade, but as he was absent, the band went to the residence of Alderman Jaeger, mayor pro tem, and gave him the municipal honors. Mayor Jaeger entertained his visitors and returned with them to the gardens, where he was still further honored.

Another incident of the day worthy of record was the execution of some fine music by the Germania and city bands in unison, to the delight of the large number of those present.

Altogether the day passed most pleasantly and profitably. The receipts, we learn, were $1,841.80. The expenses will not exceed $200.

The Casino (1901)

The "Casino" was built in 1901 at 1600 White Street, and became the center of social and educational activities for the parish and the community. This building was a dream of Father Johannes who wanted a building to serve as the "vitality of the parish." (Sigwarth, 1967)

There were meetings rooms for the various societies of the parish including the St. Boniface Young Men's Society, the St. John's Youth Group, which had about 200 members, the Sodality and the Men's Catholic Order of Foresters.

The Casino also served the recreational needs of the community. A bowling alley, with two lanes was located along the north side of the hall in the basement. A billiards room was located on the main floor along with a room for men to play their favorite card games. The gymnasium, though small, was in the basement. The building also contained a kitchen and dining room. (Silent Classroom, 1959)

The jewel of the building was the theatre complete with horseshoe balcony and seating capacity for 700. The state had three front curtains, eight backdrops and eleven sets of scenery. Tremendous plays were performed their including "Rome Under Valerian," "Quo Vadis" and "The Upper Room." All were produced in proper costume and setting. (Sigwarth, 1967)

Prior to the depression, Father Zeyen oversaw updates to the facilities of the rectory and the Casino. He had the theatre floor and the horseshoe balcony removed so the auditorium could be used for basketball instead.

> *Memories of St. Mary's would not be complete without those of St. Mary's Casino. It was the social and meeting center of St. Mary's Parish and included two basketball courts, two bowling alleys [lanes] and a recreation room having a pool and billiard table.*
>
> *It also housed the 5th grade girls' school room. In those days the boys and girls were separated from the 5th through 8th grades. Most of all it acted as a young boys' recreational center for the St. Mary's area. My father, Adolph, during*

the mid 1930s to mid 1940s, was the custodian and caretaker. During that period I spent my boyhood helping him and enjoying the facilities. Some of the families of the area I remember as I grew up were the Bannons, Kamentz, Purnages, Ernsdorff, Moran, Hickey, and Spautz. The family fathers would tell my dad, "Adolph, if my boys misbehave, let me know." My dad never had a problem. The Casino lives in the memories of those that were involved at the time, unfortunately, along came December 7, 1941. We know that the Casino Boys answered the CALL of our country. Unfortunately, some never returned.
—Al Heitzman (2010)

Convent and Jackson Street School
Contributed by St. Mary's Church Archives

Class of 1907
Contributed by St. Mary's Church Archives

St. Mary's High School for Boys (1906)

In 1906, under the tenure of Reverend Heer, the Brothers of Mary from St. Louis were invited to come to Dubuque. With their help the St. Mary's High School for Boys was opened at 1651 White Street. Across from the Casino, it was a three-year business high school aimed at preparing the students for the business world. The young men took courses that included shorthand, typing, and bookkeeping along with liberal arts courses necessary for entrance into college. (Silent Classroom, 1959)

The high school was popular with the public and business owners. The graduates were easily able to find employment.

Excerpt from 1918 St. Mary's Parish Directory:

RATES

The rates for a term of one year, in the High School Department are as follows:
First year.........$30.00
Second year........$40.00
Third year.........$50.00

DISCIPLINE

The discipline is firm, mild and paternal, and appeals chiefly to the pupil's conscience and sense of honor. Its aim is to form the student into an honest, upright, conscientious, and God-fearing young gentleman. Habits of industry and thoroughness of work are insisted upon. To this end every student is required to devote an average of two hours each evening to his written tasks and to the study of the prescribed lessons.

Prior to the Great Depression, the high school students were using rooms in the Casino due to lack of room in the high school building. The grade school was also filled beyond capacity and students were having classes in temporary rooms adjacent to the convent.

The school had been open 22 years but after discussions between Archbishop James Keane and Father Zeyen, the high school was closed. Some of the students in need would be subsidized at Loras Academy. The upper grade boys would transfer from the Jackson Street School and use classrooms at the high school building. The class of 1929 was the last to graduate. At the time, the decision to close was not well received but later history would prove it was for the best.

Immaculate Conception Academy for Girls (1907)

The Immaculate Conception Academy for girls was opened in 1907. It was originally located on 17th and Iowa Streets but was moved on September 9, 1925, to Davis Street to what is now the Shalom Retreat Center.

Excerpt from 1918 St. Mary's Parish Directory:

> The prime purpose of the Academy is to impart to young ladies a substantial education and to assist them in forming their character to make them courteous and useful members in society.
>
> The institution provides for the following departments: The Preparatory, giving a thorough training in the grammar grades; the Academic, affording a complete high school course of our years; the Commercial, including a thorough course in Bookkeeping and Stenography; the Normal, for students preparing to take teachers' examinations, and the Department of Music and Elocution; each and every department being complete in itself. The Commercial Course embodies the practical methods of Phonography, Typewriting and Bookkeeping. In the Department of Music, students will be taught vocal and instrumental, as well as Harmony, and every advantage is offered to develop the talent of the pupil.

The Academy was eventually moved to Mount St. Francis and in 1959, the Academy closed when Wahlert Catholic High School opened. The building is now the Shalom Retreat Center.

St. Mary's High School,
Contributed by St. Mary's Church Archives

Original Immaculate Conception Academy
Photo © 2010, Candice Chaloupka

St. Mary's High School, Class of 1924
Contributed by St. Mary's Church Archives

TELEGRAPH HERALD

May 26, 2009

Academies Evoke Fond Memories after 50 Years
By Mary Nevans-Pederson TH Staff Writer

Fifty years ago this month, graduations at four Dubuque high schools were melancholy and bittersweet. They would be the last classes to graduate from Immaculate Conception Academy, St. Joseph Academy, St. Columbkille High School, and Loras Academy.

As aging Catholic high schools became too expensive to repair and maintain, officials of the Archdiocese of Dubuque decided to close them and build a new, state-of-the-art high school for all of the city's parochial students to attend.

Wahlert High School opened its doors in the fall of 1959, welcoming students from the four Catholic academies that closed. Former students from each school shared some memories.

Not many people return to live in their former high schools, but Sister Carol Hemesath did and declares it a "wonderful" experience.

The Dubuque Franciscan sister was a 1955 graduate of Immaculate Conception Academy, now Shalom Retreat Center and residential apartments. Hemesath and two other sisters live in what was once the auditorium of the all-girls school. "I loved my high school. It was a time to blossom, and I took advantage of it," said Hemesath, 71.

The "beautiful friendships and the happiness" she saw in her Franciscan teachers made a lasting impression on Hemesath, who joined the Sisters of St. Francis directly out of high school, trading her navy blue wool school uniform for a religious habit. Studying music and being part of all the academy's music groups served her well, leading to a long career as a music teacher.

Every year, several hundred former "I. C." students show up at reunions to recall favorite memories like dancing the jitterbug during lunch time while a talented student played popular songs on the dining room piano.

© 2009 *Telegraph Herald*. Reprinted with permission.

1930s

Father Zeyen's tenure was during tough economic times for St. Mary's and all of Dubuque. Banks failed and there were now many who were poor in the city. Father Heer saw to the needs and fed the crowds that came to the back door of the rectory. Students fell asleep during class because they did not have breakfast so Father Zeyen bought milk for them. Long before the government began a hot lunch program, Father Zeyen began providing free hot lunch for the children who could not afford any.

> *Our class would walk to Loras to attend programs. For the last day of school we would have a picnic at Eagle Point Park.*
> —Sisters Mary Ann Wagner and Corinne Kutsch (2010)

Class of 1934 with Father Frommelt
Contributed by St. Mary's Church Archives

1940s

Monsignor Klott, organized a program for the Catholic children of Dubuque who were in special classes at Prescott School. He invited students to come to Rohlman Hall for weekly religion classes. These students needed more individual attention so the teacher/student ratio was kept small at 1:5. This program was in effect for over 20 years.

The former building for St. Mary's High School for boys on White Street was sold due to a drop in school enrollment after the depression. At that time, the number of students had dropped to below 500.

> *I have always been impressed that in the 1940s and early 1950s at least it was an entirely free school, no tuition. The only charge was a $5.00 annual book rental fee. There were also no student fund-raising efforts apparently needed; no candy sales, raffles, etc.*
>
> *Looking back, it is amazing to think that Sister Canisia, now residing at Holy Family Hall, taught all academic subjects AND provided guidance, taking a personal interest in her eighth graders AND had the responsibilities of school principal AND, I believe, was the local superior. I often saw appreciative former students return to talk and consult with her.* —David A. Vanderah (2010)
>
> *Every grade would do something for the priest, probably to celebrate his Feast Day or birthday. One year the first graders dressed in their pajamas and had a pillow fight; second graders dressed like graduates and did a story about graduating; the third graders had a doll store and dressed like dolls.*
>
> *After the performances, the priest would announce that the next day was a "free day" which meant No School!*
> —Sr. Marie Therese Kalb (2010)

1941–1944 Class with Fathers Nereser, Zeyen and Steinlage
Contributed by St. Mary's Church Archives

1950s

Once again the Jackson Street School building was too small to provide enough classrooms and the Casino, the once popular center of social activity was no longer the icon it had been. Television and automobiles increased options for entertainment, so families found other ways to amuse themselves. The large building was now considered a "white elephant."

It was decided to completely remove the interior of the Casino to build new classrooms. The building was covered with porcelainized aluminum (considered modern for the time) in St. Mary's colors of blue and white. This modernization also made the building fire-proof so it received a top insurance rating.

After complete renovation, the building became the new St. Mary's School and was dedicated to educating children on April 5, 1959. (Parish history 1849–2000)

With the new building, the school enrollment, including a kindergarten rose to the all time high of 808 students in 1960. The new and improved Casino was now an integral part of the school — providing eight classrooms, an administrative office, a nurse's office, library, auditorium, and gymnasium. The basement became a multipurpose dining room with a well-equipped kitchen

The Casino after Remodel (The Blue Building)
Contributed by St. Mary's Church Archives

which served both the school and the social needs for the adults. (Sigwarth, 1967)

The auditorium stage was equipped with a high fidelity sound system and a four-color lighting system which was very useful for the many assemblies and play productions.

An intercom and radio system allowed Principal Sister Mary Angelita, OSF, contact with all of the classrooms in both the old Jackson Street school building and the new building. This also allowed for recorded and live radio programs to be broadcasted in the classrooms for educational purposes. (Silent Classroom, 1959)

In a newspaper article, source unknown, Sister M. Anita, OSF, who taught at St. Mary's from 1905 to 1942, recalled her 38 years there. Twelve of her former students became priests and three became sisters. "There would have been more sisters," She explained, "but I didn't start teaching girls until the Brothers of Mary left St. Mary's in 1929."

Sister Anita also recalled a year when Father Rohlman was still the assistant:

I told him that we just had too many students and couldn't properly handle them all. Father told me the only way to cut down was to take out some seats. So, sure enough, out came the front rows and those that couldn't be seated had to go elsewhere.

I'll never forget the day we had a fire at St. Mary's, she recalled. It was a dry September day in 1920 or '21. We had just come from church to the classroom.

Suddenly we heard the sound of screaming fire engines and all of the boys jumped up and raced to the window. I told them to return to their places immediately. It never entered my mind that the school was on fire.

Then there was a hurried knock on the door and I went over to see who it was. There stood an excited fireman. "Hurry Sister, get the boys out, the roof's on fire!"

By the time I got turned around the classroom as empty. There was a fire escape right by the window, and before I had a chance to say anything they were all on the ground looking up at the fire!
(Silent Classroom, 1959)

The years passed by so quickly. It has been fifty-five years since the St. Mary's graduating 8th graders of 1955 went their separate ways. But, we never had to say goodbye. The bond created from our grade school friendships way back when roller skating, Ricky Nelson, and nickel bags of chips were king, lives on today. I will be forever grateful for my friends from St. Mary's who have formed a lunch club. Joanne Mootz, Karen Kelly, Lois Shetler, Carol Dougherty, and I get together about once a monthly to reminisce about the good 'ole days. Friendships sometimes come and go.

However, these friendships formed in the 1950s, have stood the test of time. Like my memories of St. Mary's, they will last forever.
—Ann Klaus (2010)

Class of 1955
Contributed by St. Mary's Church Archives

Wahlert High School

The renovations to the Casino were done at the same time as the building of Wahlert High School. Each Parish in Dubuque was to share in the cost of building it with St. Mary's portion coming to $330,000. The total cost for Wahlert and the renovated school building was over $700,000, leaving the parish in debt in the amount of $224,000.

Hot Lunch

Father Sigwarth reports in the Centennial brochure that St. Mary's had a hot lunch program for over 15 years with 400 children making use of the program as of 1967. The program was in large part due to the volunteer efforts of 32 women who divided the responsibility so that there was a group of ladies available for each day of the week. "The volunteers make it possible to put money into protein instead of labor."

St. Mary's was my most favorite teaching assignment. I came there as a new, very young (20) Sister just out of the Novitiate. I was assigned to teach second grade with Sister Mary Oda. One of my most memorable events was time for First Holy Communion. We marched all around the block before entering the church. Some of the children would try to blow out the small candles in the back of church as we entered. To this day, in 2010, I still come in contact with students from that time and they always remember me. They were delightful.

Another memorable event was when Father Sigwarth handed out the children's report cards. This took place where the parking lot is now by the old convent. There was a bit of fear in the air as he was quite strict.

After a few years, when the new school on White Street was opened, the first grade teachers, Sister Marna and Sister Cynthia (who had been teaching first grade in the church basement) moved into that building along with the upper grades.

When those two sisters moved from St. Mary's, I was delighted to move to teaching first grade and in the "blue" school. In a couple of years over there Sister Patrick Mary (now Yvonne McKeon) was assigned to teach with me. We had the most memorable years of my teaching. For a couple of years we each had 53 first graders in our classroom.

Sister Cecil was principal and she was wonderful. I remember when our rooms would be half full due to flu, etc., we would each take the whole class and give the other a break. Millie Heiderscheit was the lead cook in the cafeteria and she would call us down and give us chocolate chip cookies. We loved her! She loved the two of us!

At the time I was at St. Mary's we were 18 sisters. I remember we walked across the parking lot as a group to attend Mass/Services in church and we always sat in the front two rows.

After I left St. Mary's, I returned several summers as Lead Teacher at the Head Start Program. We used the cafeteria of the "blue" school. Different sisters assisted me and also some St. Mary's mothers and students. It was a great experience.

I will never forget St. Mary's and I am grateful to our congregation for allowing me to minister there as a young sister. I call it "the good ole days." The people in the parish were so friendly and kind and even though many were so very poor. They were good to the sisters. I have always kept St. Mary's families in my daily prayers.
—Sister Carolyn Thirtle (2010)

Sister Mary Edith Ann, 1961
Contributed by Sr. Carolyn Thirtle

Sister Mary Edith Ann and 1967 Headstart Class
Contributed by Sr. Carolyn Thirtle

Sister Mary Edith Ann and Sister Lila, Headstart Class 1967
Contributed by Sr. Carolyn Thirtle

1980s

Despite the efforts of the sisters, lay teachers, parents and generosity of the parishioners, the school that had remained opened for 150 years was closing. In 1982, the decision was made to combine St. Mary's School and St. Patrick's School since both were feeling the effects of dwindling enrollments. Children of the parish would have to attend the newly formed Downtown Catholic Elementary School. Kindergarten and fifth through eighth grades attended classes at the St. Patrick's building while grades one through four attended at the St. Mary's building.

After a couple of years, the name was changed from Downtown Catholic to St. Mary/St. Patrick Grade School in response to continued requests of the local families.

The school started as a place for German-immigrant children and evolved into an institution that met the needs of children from all ethnicities. In the last decades the members played a major role in welcoming and embracing the ethnically diverse persons who came to Dubuque.

The enrollment at St. Mary/St. Patrick Grade School continued to decline so plans were made to merge into one site. Heating problems at the St. Mary building forced the issue and in March 1999, all students were housed at the St. Patrick site.

2000s

In the fall of 2001, the Holy Family Catholic School Board proposed combining St. Mary's/St. Patrick's with Holy Trinity/Sacred Heart School. Enrollment in the Holy Family Catholic School system had been dropping, with the most loss coming from St. Mary's/St. Patrick's and Holy Trinity/Sacred Heart Schools. So in May of 2002, all four parish schools combined and became St. Francis School. (Bowerman, 2004) It remained open until June of 2004. (Itza Heim, email message to author, April 26, 2010)

Letter from the Archives of the
Sisters of St. Francis of the Holy Family

```
     As the school year ends, we extend the thanks of
the parish to the Sisters, lay Teachers, Aides, and
the many volunteers that assisted in the operation
of the school this past year. Thanks also to Father
Moore and all those who taught and assisted in the CCD
program for 1981-82.
     The last class graduated from St. Mary's School
on May 28, 1982. Saint Mary's School ceased to exist
as a separate entity on June 2, 1982, ending a
tradition of 133 years of Catholic education in
St. Mary's Parish. The tradition of Catholic Education
for the children of St. Mary's will continue in
the new Downtown Catholic Elementary School in
participation with St. Patrick's Parish. May it too
have a long and illustrious history!
```

A number of sisters have lived at St. Mary's since the school closed, and been involved in the parish, e.g., Marge Staudt, Josephine Schmitz, Carol Hoverman. Lucille Lammers played funerals there until shortly before her death last year. (Sisters of St. Francis Archives)

> *Of the many sisters that taught at St. Mary's, most of them had St. Maryitis when they left. It had gotten into their blood. One of them never left. Sister Mary Damien came to St. Mary's from the novitiate in 1904; she spent 48 years here; and died at her desk in one of the classrooms in 1952.* (Sigwarth, 1967)

> *A Sr. Damien saying: "The mills of God grind slowly, but they grind exceedingly fine."* — David A. Vanderah (2010)

Class of 1955
Contributed by St. Mary's Church Archives

Sister Damien was the sixth grade teacher forever. In 1949–50, she seemed quite old to me, but that is the way with young people toward elders. She trained acolytes as part of her duties, I believe, and thus must have taught us church Latin for mass responses. I recall her showing the class an old "fiddleback" chasuble, with maniple and stole. It seemed worn, like her. I can see her fingers stroking the material, perhaps thinking of former liturgical garb days or wanting to impress the boys with fancy priestly vestments.
— David A. Vanderah (2010)

The most wonderful years of my life were spent at St. Mary's. The faculty was like a family. We had a great sisters community where Sr. Kathleen made a home for us. The people were so appreciative and cooperative. It was during these years that we began faith communities.
—Sr. Rita Green (2010)

[Sr. Rita Green was the Principal at St. Mary's from 1968–1980.]

Some dates and events in the history of Catholic Education at St. Mary's:

1849 – The first school was opened in the basement of Holy Trinity Church (predecessor of St. Mary's) on 8th & White, with lay teachers.

1852 – The Sisters of Charity of the Blessed Virgin Mary took over the operation of the school.

1869 – Franciscan Sisters of Perpetual Adoration (LaCrosse, WI) come to teach at St. Mary's.

1872 – New St. Mary's School on Jackson Street opens.

1879 – Franciscan Sisters of the Holy Family take over St. Mary's School, beginning a 103-year association with the school.

1906 – St. Mary's High School for Boys was opened, with the Brothers of Mary conducting the school. Tuition was $30 for the first year, $40 for year two, and $50 for year three. Payments could be made in advance or monthly for 10 months. It was closed in 1928.

1907 – St. Mary's was instrumental in the establishment of the first Immaculate Conception Academy for girls on 17th Street.

1956 – St. Mary's joins with the other parishes of Dubuque to establish Wahlert High School.

1959 – St. Mary's Casino is converted into the White Street School.

1960 – St. Mary's reaches a peak enrollment of 808 students.

1982 – May 28 – Last graduating class from St. Mary's.
June 2 – St. Mary's School closes and becomes a part of the new Downtown Catholic Elementary School.

—Contributed by Sisters of St. Francis Archives

TELEGRAPH HERALD

November 21, 2001

Holy Family Discusses Budget Plan: 'Short-term fix?': Six speak out against proposed merger of elementary schools
By Diane Heldt, TH Staff Writer

Parents and parish members from Holy Trinity/Sacred Heart are concerned about a proposal that would merge the school with St. Mary's/St. Patrick's.

Six people addressed the Board of Education of Holy Family Catholic Schools Tuesday night; all of them were from Holy Trinity/Sacred Heart and spoke against the proposed merger.

The board met at Wahlert High School and presented its proposed 2002-03 budget, which includes several restructuring ideas and expense reductions that would cover an expected $416,000 shortfall in the system's $15 million budget. About 50 people attended the meeting.

The proposal would combine Holy Trinity/Sacred Heart and St. Mary's/St. Pat's into one school, with one principal. Grades kindergarten through four would be at the Holy Trinity/Sacred Heart building, and grades five through eight would be at the St. Mary's/St. Pat's building.

Don Miller, chief executive officer of the Holy Family system, said of the 16 classes citywide that have 13 or fewer students, 10 of them are at those two schools. Enrollment in the Holy Family system dropped 258 students this year; of that loss, 146 students were from Holy Trinity/Sacred Heart and St. Mary's/St. Pat's.

Holy Trinity/Sacred Heart parents said they expect enrollment at that school would drop even more if the merger is approved.

"The majority of people feel that this proposal is a very short-term fix that will drive away scores of people from the downtown and north end Catholic schools," said parent Jeff Streinz.

Parents said they don't like that the proposal would split children between fourth and fifth grade, leaving one building with younger children. They said more support might be gathered for a plan that would leave kindergarten through sixth grade together in one building.

"I do believe most of our parents will not accept this and will probably move to another school if the proposal is approved," said parent Randy Hohnecker.

There's also concern that even with the merger and other measures, the system won't be able to save enough money to keep the budget balanced, especially if enrollment drops again, the speakers said.

"Will we be in the same situation next year, doing this all over again?" asked Sacred Heart parishioner Frank Miller.

Holy Family board President Brian Kane said the board is not trying to "ramrod" through any plans.

"All the comments will be listened to respectfully and considered," he said. "We constantly focus as a board on our mission and these core components of Catholic education. We all need to continue to work together on this."

The proposed Holy Family budget also would cut 18.7 full-time staff positions — 8 or 8 1/2 of them at Wahlert High School, to help reduce costs.

The Holy Family board will vote on the budget at its Dec. 18 meeting.

© 2009 *Telegraph Herald*. Reprinted with permission.

Two special memories from my years of teaching music at St. Mary's were the musicals put on by the junior high students. I particularly remember Tom Sawyer *and* The Wizard of Oz. *With* Tom Sawyer, *I will always remember how Tim Voels as Tom Sawyer and Bobbie Freese as Huck Finn sat on the edge of the stage holding this stuffed "dead cat" and when one of them said —"It's sure stiff, isn't it," the other got laughing so hard that the audience laughed hysterically at them. With* Wizard of Oz, *everyone seems to remember Barb Caldwell as the witch screeching — "I'm melting, I'm melting" when the "water" was thrown on her.*
—Sr. Carol Hoverman (2010)

Flowers in Alice in Wonderland, circa 1983–1984
Contributed by Young/Walsh Family

*7th Grade Class, Downtown Catholic Elementary, 1983–1984
Sister Lucy Kurt and Steve Cornelius, Principals
Mr. Dagget, Teacher*
Contributed by Young/Walsh Family

Mr. Dagget was the 7th grade science teacher. One evening after school he came to the office, and mentioned his snake [boa constrictor] was missing. The next morning, as I was making the announcements over the PA to both the Jackson and White Street Schools, a scream erupted behind me in the office, and was carried over the PA to the whole school. The secretary, Carolyn, had been typing at her desk, and dropped a sheet of paper between the desk and wall. As she pulled out the desk, there lay the snake. Mr. Dagget came running up the hall, " I think they found my snake."
—Sr. Rita Green (2010)

There was a "Fun Day" which was held during the middle of May each year. The students were responsible for setting up and tearing down the booths where students could play games. The day ended with a drawing for prizes. Chances were five cents each. The grand prize was usually a bicycle. The teachers would stand on the porch of the Sisters' convent and draw names. —Sr. Rita Green (2010)

The Fun Days at St. Mary's were the best, cotton candy machines, hay rides; they had it all when you're a kid. I remember a month before, they would have us kids going door-to-door selling chances to win items that they had donated to them, and for every 20 chances I believe you sold, your name got put in for a separate drawing. And I remember one year I won the top prize which was a ten-speed bike. I was So Happy!! —Michelle Young (2010)

I don't remember if the eclipse happened in the fall or spring of my 4th grade, but I remember going outside with the teachers with white index card with a pinhole in it. Our teachers repeatedly told us to NOT look directly at the sun, but look the pinhole, or else we would go blind!

While at St. Mary's there were two school buildings, the old one for first through fifth grades and the blue building [The Casino] for kindergarten and sixth through eighth grades. This building also had the gym, library, and lunchroom. I was in the old building and everyone looked forward to being able to go to classes in the blue building. The year I was supposed to start there, St. Mary's and St. Pat's combined into Downtown Catholic and the upper grades went to St. Pat's. I was devastated; I had waited years to go to the blue building! —Candice Chaloupka (2010)

4th Grade Class with teacher Sister Josephine Schmitz, 1980–1981
Contributed by Young/Walsh Family

Thank you to all the teachers and staff
who faithfully educated the thousands of students
that attended St. Mary's School!

L to R: *Emil Schneider, Frank John Schneider, Amelia Schneider, Hilda Schneider, Louis (Capesius) Schneider*
Photo Contributed by Kirschbaum/Ralph Family

Front porch of Schneider Home at 1110 Jackson St.
Photo Contributed by Kirschbaum/Ralph Family

People of St. Mary's

It is easy to forget that a Church is its people not its structure. While St. Mary's Church is no longer functioning as a parish in Dubuque, it is not true to believe that it has died. That will not be true so long as the hundreds of former members' memories remain.

This chapter is meant to preserve the true splendor of St. Mary's — her people. Some stories are common and unpresumptuous, others may inspire or uplift, all honor God who provided this spiritual home.

A debt of gratitude is owed to the founding members of St. Mary's as well as to those who went on to faithfully serve the church and community through their membership.

Pictured within this chapter are two of the founding families: the Gotlieb Shneider family and the Henry Baule family. According to Dubuque Franciscan legend, (no documentation supports this) the Baule's opened their home to the Sisters of Mount St. Francis when they first came to Dubuque.

As providence would have it, the last day the church office was open, Mr. Kirschbaum called and informed the author his great-great-great grandfather Gotlieb Schneider was a founding member of St. Mary's in Dubuque and had helped carve the altar. Mr. Kirschbaum also shared that Gotlieb formed a cooperative of

German carpenters in Dubuque called the "Dubuque Cabinet Makers Association." In 1904, the Association became known as the present-day Spahn & Rose Lumber Company. The Spahn family were also founding members.

> *My Great-grandparents, John Duehr and Susanna Klein were childhood sweethearts in Trier, Germany. John came to the United States in 1867 or 1868, and settled in the Waupeton, Iowa area of Dubuque County. Susanna arrived in the USA in 1870, and came directly to Dubuque. The couple were married in St. Mary's Catholic Church on July 7, 1870, by Father Sauter. They became the parents of nine children who survived beyond infancy, four girls and five boys. One of the younger sons, Peter, was studying to be a priest but died at the age of 17.*
>
> *John was a learned man who taught religion, sometimes taught school, and was the local medical help for the early settlers. One of my mother's older sisters remembered the large medical books in his home which were kept high on a shelf and no one, especially the younger ones were allowed to touch, much less look at. He often was called for illness, when someone was dying, and also was called by the local midwives when there was a difficult labor and birth. Although John died when my mother was only eight years of age, his daughter, my grandmother, who lived to be 95, made her home with my parents for almost 30 years and told much of this to my mother. When her siblings would come to visit they would talk of their parents and tell of family life in the late 1800s. I grew up hearing all of the family history.*
>
> *Something I found interesting about the family is that, for the daughters, they used the German naming custom of giving the girls two names. The first was the spiritual, saint's name, and the second the secular or call name, which is the name the person was known by, both within*

family and everywhere else. In this case the five daughters (one died in infancy) all had the first name of Mary.
—Marilyn Lawrence (2010)

John and Susan Duehr
Photo Contributed by Lawrence Family

Peter Duehr
Photo Contributed by Lawrence Family

Henry and Maggie Baule, other two persons unknown
Photos Contributed by Sisters of Mount St. Francis

Generosity

St. Mary's Church members have historically been very generous in helping the poor thru donations to the poor box for St. Vincent de Paul Society. At the rear of the church there is an approximately six-foot statute of St. Vincent de Paul. My understanding many years ago St. Mary's parishioners built five poor boxes in the church at each of the five entrances. There is a small picture of St. Vincent de Paul at each location. There is an approximate six-inch diameter metal cylinder tube with a slot on the top of the tube where people could place their money. This tube went down into the basement of the church into a wooden box. Each of these five boxes were kept locked. Once a month when the St. Mary's St. Vincent de Paul committee met on Sunday morning, these boxes were unlocked and the money was collected. This money was then used to give out food vouchers to local grocery stores to the poor and disadvantaged in the St. Mary's geographic area. —Dave Becker (2010)

St. Vincent de Paul
Photo © 2009, Don Long, Jr.

The sisters kept clothes at the school for the poor children so they would have decent clothes to wear. They would change into them when they got to school and then put their own clothes back on before returning home. The poor families mainly came from across the tracks — called the flats. One of the poor families died in a fire and a communion dress was donated to bury the little girl in.
—Sister Corinne Kutsch (2010)

Tramps would come from the trains to our door begging for food. One Christmas morning one knocked at our door and my father fed him. He told us the tramp "could have been Jesus." —Sister Mary Ann Wagner (2010)

Celebrations

Turkey Fest was held every year near Thanksgiving. Paddle wheels, great tasting turkey and dressing sandwiches, and much parish hospitality and friendship.
—Dave Becker (2010)

The following pictures are from the Cluster Picnics held at Jackson Park on August 1, 2004, and Murphy Park in 2009.

Photos taken by Mary Ostrander
Contributed by St. Mary's Church Archives

Father Ardel Barta
Photos taken by Mary Ostrander
Contributed by St. Mary's Church Archives

Fathers Eugene Kutsch, Steve Rosonke, Monsignor John Friedel and Ron Friedel
Photos taken by Mary Ostrander
Contributed by St. Mary's Church Archives

Father Steve Rosonke Prays before Meal
Photos taken by Mary Ostrander
Contributed by St. Mary's Church Archives

First Communion

The day is a warm and sunny day in May 1951. Outside St. Mary's Church there is about 44 angelic children all dressed in white awaiting for the signal to begin the procession into church to make our First Holy Communion.

During the previous week we all made the Sacrament of Penance — boy was there a lot of long sad faces in that line. After we finished with the holy sacrament the faces looked to be calming and peaceful. The rest of that week the teachers and parents had the best behaved children because we were not going to take the chance of not making our Holy Communion.

Saturday night at my house was very busy. I was the first one to get to bathe because mom had to put my hair up in rag curls. Before retiring I bet I was told by every adult in the house not to drink any water after midnight. To make sure this wouldn't happen my mom tied rags around every faucet in the house even after I prayed to God for help in this matter.

Sunday morning dawned beautiful and sunny. Mom brushed out my curls and I didn't even grumble because I knew this was my special day. The last thing I got to put on was my white dress. I had the reputation to step out my door and the dirt attached to me like glue. Mom always said I would step outside the door and say "dirt, here I am." To be on the safe side, mom walked on one side of me and dad on the other. They were going to get me to church in my clean white dress.

When my turn came to receive Holy Communion I stepped forward with dignity and pride. I think I was almost as tall as the rest of the kids in my class instead of the shortest. After receiving my host and returning to my pew I said a special prayer to Jesus, "Lord if the world is coming to an end, please let it happen today so I can come directly to you before I have a chance to misbehave." Needless to say the world did not end on May 1951.

My dress stayed in a plastic bag sealed to prevent discoloration until I had my first daughter and then I made it into a christening dress for her and the rest of my girls wore it also. —Mary Ostrander (2010)

When a newly ordained priest celebrated his first Mass, there was a custom that a young girl would dress like a bride, representing the church. She would carry the burse, *the fabric that held the Corporal placed over the chalice. I was the "bride" for my oldest brother's first mass which was said at St. Mary's. During the dinner at the Casino after the mass, I read a poem the 8th grade teacher helped me memorize. We practiced during recess.*

My second and third oldest brothers also celebrated their first Masses at St. Mary's. My parents' funeral was held at St. Mary's. —Sister Marie Therese Kalb (2010)

The Crowning of the May Queen was an important day. The First Communicants would wear their Communion dresses and a special crown was put on the head of the Blessed Mary statute and the rosary was said by those attending the celebration. —Sister Mary Ann Wagner and Sister Corinne Kutsch (2010)

Mary Ostrander, May 1951
Photo Contributed by Mary Ostrander

Baptismal Font
Photo © 2009, Don Long, Jr

I was baptized at St. Mary's in July, 1938. I am familiar with all parts of it from the baptistry, confessionals, fonts, the decoratively painted walls, the sanctuary steps, the vestry, even remembering the spotless white houseling cloth I pulled over to cover the rail when accompanying the priest as he placed the host on the tongues of parishioners.
—David A. Vanderah (2010)

I came to St. Mary's in 1925, when I was six-months-old with my parents, Bernard and Mary (Schaetzle) Vonderheide, and six-year-old brother, Joseph.

I made my First Communion and Confirmation, graduating from grade school and continued on with the Franciscan nuns to the Immaculate Conception Academy. I married Floyd Heying at St. Mary's and was married for 37 years when he passed away. Later I married Bern Hillary at St. Mary's and we've been together 23 years.

Christmas was my favorite holy day — seeing the beautiful crib and going to midnight mass with my mother. Forty

Hours was a beautiful service with all the red roses and our beautiful gold altar. I feel sad to leave St. Mary's after attending the church for 85 years.
—Betty (Vonderheide) Hillary (2010)

Baptismal Font
Photo © 2009, Don Long, Jr.

St. Mary's Nativity
Photo contributed by St. Mary's Church Archives

Christmas

Christmas is a special time of year, we celebrate the birth of our Savior and Lord, and although St. Mary's was always beautiful, at Christmas time it was grand.

Christmas Eve, 1945
After supper, my mother took me on a walk through our neighborhood to look at the Christmas light displays. When we reached 15th Street, St. Mary's looked dark against a sky full of stars. It was chilly and a light snow fell on us as we walked. On the way back to our corner of 12th and Washington, we passed homes some with blue star banners and one with a gold star, reminders of the war just ended in August. It was quiet, as we made our way past Rink's Market, like most businesses closed early for Christmas Eve.

At home, Dad had untangled the lights and set up the tree and creche. My parents, my brother Don, and I listened

to the radio broadcast of "A Christmas Carol." Then we exchanged gifts and prepared for church. Our Christmas Eve walk to see the holiday lights became a tradition.
—David A. Vanderah (2010)

I come from a family of five kids and when we were younger, we lived across the street from St. Mary's Church. We went to church every Saturday but the Christmas Eve Mass was the longest for us because we knew once the Mass was over with, we got to open up our Christmas gifts that we waited all year for. But it never failed, once Church got over with, somebody would lock their keys in their car and the nice guy my dad is, he would always help. That meant longer for us to open up our gifts and you know when you're a kid that's like forever!
—Michelle Young (2010)

During the Christmas season each year there is a large wooden crib with a shingled roof set up at the front of the church on the St. Joseph side. The crib was made by St. Mary's Parishioners, Frank Reinert and Joe Ungs. It had large Nativity cene statues and a lighted sign reading; Gloria in Excelsis Deo. It is probably one of the largest indoor church cribs anywhere.
—Dave Becker (2010)

When I was a little girl, (this would have been the 1970s) I was one of the children who was a part of the processional that carried the baby Jesus and gifts to the nativity scene set up at the front of the church. But that's not why I remember this service. This was a special service because KDUB-TV news came. At that time, Gary Dolphin was the anchorman and that was the news channel my father watched every night. I had a crush on Gary Dolphin and was excited to see a person who was on TV because at that time, I believed anyone on TV was famous.
—Candice Chaloupka (2010)

Christmas Eve

When the fever of shopping is over;
When the lights on the tree have been tried;
When our love for our friends has been gift-wrapped,
And the ribbons have all been tied;

Let me pause for a spell from the turmoil,
On this night of all nights of the year,
Let me tune into Bethlehem's station
And drink in the message clear.

Let me listen to Mary who lullabies
The precious Prince of Peace to sleep-
No drums of war to disturb His rest
And Joseph there the guard to keep.

With shepherds who heard the News on the hill
And saw the dark night turn to noon,
Let me read by the light of celestial skies
God's message as I commune.

For let me not miss the glory and bliss,
Spilled to earth on this night so sublime
When heaven beams down to country and town
The greatest broadcast of all time.
—Msgr. Anthony W. Sigwarth

Looking Up
Photo © 2010, Candice Chaloupka

The Steeple
You cannot look down on St. Mary's
Its steeple towers so high:
In sun and in moonlight and weather,
It seems to commune with the sky.

The secrets it snatches from heaven
May it share with this town and its people,
Who toil here with hope in the valley
And look up with joy to the steeple.
—Msgr. Anthony W. Sigwarth

Venerable Doorstep

The doorstep beneath this grand tower
Is worn down one inch and a half;
Feet ground it in search of God's Power;
It was tapped by the Archbishop's staff.
beneath the magnificent steeple,
Beyond the worn step that men trod,
Stretch vistas of beauty which people
Have fashioned in love for their God.

In this house of our God and His people
May God's grace be showered on men;
And may grateful souls, like the steeple,
Reach upward to heaven. Amen
—Msgr. Anthony W. Sigwarth

Beloved St. Mary's

I have seen the cathedrals of Europe;
I have prayed at the shrines of the world;
But I love to come back to St. Mary's
And see here such great things unfurled.

Here heaven and earth have a wedding;
Here weakness with grace is made strong;
Eternity drops down its secrets,
Here history has written a song.

—Msgr. Anthony W. Sigwarth

Banner at Back of Church
Photo © 2009, Don Long, Jr.

View from the Loft
Photo © 2009, Don Long, Jr.

Be Proud of St. Mary's
It could fittingly stand and honor command
Along streets of Milan and Cologne.
On England's Isle, it could tourists beguile
As a Cathedral widely known.
In Ireland fair, I feel that there
It would be a beloved shrine.
So wherever you roam, come proudly back home
To this beautiful church of thine.
—Msgr. Anthony W. Sigwarth

*Thank you Heavenly Father for having
blessed us so well and for so long.
Amen.*

Father Steve Rosonke and Members Celebrating the Mass
Photo © 2010, Sr. Carol Hoverman, OSF

The Closing

In the summer of 2009, St. Mary's graced the cover of several issues of the Telegraph Herald. Unfortunately it was because the Pastoral Planning Committee proposed closing St. Mary's Parish.

Several factors were cited for the decision to close including: the decline in membership, dwindling contributions and involvement, coupled with current and anticipated debt, and major maintenance costs to parish buildings exceeding $2 million. (*The Witness*, August 30, 2009)

The following is a reprint of the letter sent to parishioners with the information presented at the parish meeting held on July 15, 2009.

St. Mary/St. Patrick Pastoral Planning Committee Recommendation June 25, 2009

Since March 26, 2009, the St. Mary/St. Patrick Pastoral Planning Committee (formerly the Strategic Planning Committee) has been meeting to investigate the current and future situations of the two parishes, evaluate viability, and make a recommendation to the Cluster Council as to the status of both parishes.

In 2007, the Planning Committee made a report to the Cluster Council which recommended the urgent need to take action to build both parishes for the future. This involved obtaining commitments from parishioners for their involvement in the parishes through a "covenant" and survey. Cluster committees would be formed in an effort to strengthen the community life of the parishes. Announcements were made at all Masses in both parishes and this process was continued through bulletin announcements and a variety of methods for several months.

In evaluating the results of those efforts, the present Pastoral Planning Committee agreed that the effort did not succeed at revitalizing the cluster. In fact, there was actually a diminished response in areas such as Mass attendance, committee strength, and financial stewardship. The following were found to be characteristic of the two parishes:

- Financial support continues to decline.
- Fewer young families are involved in the life of the parish.
- Baptisms, First Communions, and marriages continue to decline.
- 63% of parishioners are over 70 years of age.
- Both parishes have been dramatically affected by the changes in the neighborhood.
- About 90% of our current parishioners are living outside our parish boundaries.

It is the opinion of this committee that the overall picture of the decline of the parishes is due to trends and issues beyond anyone's control. There are specific and urgent issues that need to be addressed now, including the following:

- For the 2009-2010 fiscal year, both parishes have deficit budgets. St. Mary projects a $150,000 deficit

and St. Patrick projects a $100,000 deficit. This amounts to 20-30% of their total budgets.
- Bequests and/or money borrowed from the Archdiocese are being used to meet operating expenses. St. Mary's current debt is about $160,000.
- Major maintenance needs for St. Mary's amount to over $2,700,000.

At the same time but separate from the work of this committee, the St. Mary Finance Council reached a consensus that St. Mary is no longer financially viable. This was based on the parish's inability to meet operating expenses and the magnitude of the maintenance issues. This consensus was communicated to the Pastoral Planning Committee on June 16, 2009.

The Pastoral Planning Committee considered several options for the future. The committee looked at mission membership from other parishes, a fund raising effort, placing buildings on the Historical Register, other collaborations (Loras, Archdiocese) and recruiting new parishioners. Upon careful discussion, none of these options appeared to be feasible.

In consideration of the points listed above and particularly of the urgent financial situation for St. Mary Parish, the Pastoral Planning Committee recommends that St. Mary Parish cease operations as a parish.

There are many unknowns regarding ramifications of this recommendation. The committee felt compelled to take action and was aware that making no recommendation was not an appropriate reaction to these circumstances. It is our hope that St. Patrick will be able to sustain a parish community and serve as a Catholic presence in the neighborhood.

Respectfully submitted by
St. Mary/St. Patrick Pastoral Planning Committee

On July 7, 20009, at a special Cluster Council Meeting, St. Mary's Parish Council, St. Patrick's Parish Council, St. Mary's Finance Council, and St. Patrick's Finance Council considered and consented to this recommendation. In a closed session that evening, the St. Mary's Parish Council tentatively endorsed this recommendation.

TELEGRAPH HERALD

July 16, 2009

St. Mary's church will close: Officials say financial difficulties and a shrinking congregation contributed to the decision to close the 142-year-old parish.
By Bekah Porter, TH Staff Writer

Tears pool in Karen Birch's eyes. "We need a miracle," she says. "We need a miracle so badly." On Wednesday, Birch turned to her refuge in times of tribulation — her parish.

Miracles can happen here at St. Mary's Catholic Church in Dubuque, she says, and a nearby window showing Jesus walking from the tomb reminds her that hope can prevail. But no colored glass depicts her beloved church rising from the dead. "I hope it can, and I will pray it does," she says, "because what will I do if it doesn't?"

Reasons

About 200 parishioners gathered at St. Mary's on Wednesday to hear the announcement that they'd been dreading for days. "St. Mary's Parish will cease operations," Pastoral Associate Ann Wertz read from the pulpit. More than 142 years after the facility opened its doors, it will close.

The reasons why are numerous, church officials said. At least 63 percent of the parishioners are older than 70, and the church population dies day by day, although 600 families still are considered members of the church. Fewer young families seek the church. The neighborhood isn't Catholic anymore, and at least 90 percent of the congregation lives outside parish boundaries.

Financial problems plague the parish. St. Mary's projects a $150,000 deficit for the 2009—10 fiscal year, and current debt exceeds $150,000. Additionally, at least $2 million worth of repairs remain. Officials said there is no timeline for the closure.

Emotional Reaction

The announcement came at about 6:30 p.m. Wertz distributed handouts to the ushers, who then walked among the pews. Except for the rustling of the paper, silence dominated the chapel as church members allowed the words to become real.

Church officials made speeches, crying as they told how hard it was to make the decision to shut down the church where they had been baptized and married.

But anger surfaced. Teresa Ruzicka was the first of more than a dozen members to address the congregation, and she marched to the front of the church to interrupt the Rev. Steve Rosonke's address. To much applause, she said she was sick of hearing how older members contributed to the closing."I'm getting a little bit tired of being told I'm not viable if I'm not 35 or younger," she said.

Some speakers talked about how the Archdiocese of Dubuque seemed to thwart fundraising efforts in the past: no archdiocese representative attended the meeting and how the organization also prevented the building from being placed on the registry of historic places.

Others said they wanted to know why the church failed to ask the congregation's opinion, to which Wertz explained that the councils and committees were elected to represent the congregation."It's not a democracy," she said.

Others thanked the committee members for their decision and agreed that diminishing volunteer numbers and drooping tithes contributed to the problem.

Still, one issue incited the crowd more than any — the annual $230,000 assessment fee the church pays to the Holy Family Schools to support area Catholic education.

School Fees
For several speeches, the issue was avoided. Then one speaker said that Holy Family drove the church into debt each year, and the church roared with applause. One father of four said that the fee was unfair.

"We have been bled and bled and bled and bled, and now we're empty, and I'm sorry to say that bleeding was done by the Holy Family school system," he said. "I have four children, but I am not going to ask you guys to send them to school. That's my responsibility."

Church officials said the fee is determined based on the number of students attending Catholic schools, the number of potential students, the church's annual income and parish debt. Holy Family Catholic Schools chief administrator Steve Cornelius said that 21 students from St. Mary's are enrolled for Catholic school for this fall thus far. The bill for Catholic education is paid by parish assessments, fundraising, and tuition. For the past five years, student tuition has increased 7 percent, although parish subsidies have decreased 8.5 percent since 2005.

One mother said the fee was necessary, adding that the operating budget of St. Mary's own Catholic school, now closed, was $400,000. "I realize what we are paying now is a lot, but it's less than what it once was," she said. "I would hope my children would have the same right to a Catholic education that you and your children had."

In Need of Prayer
More than two hours after the meeting started, parishioners began streaming from beneath the steeple that is reportedly the highest in the entire Mississippi River Valley.

Just as they had done Sunday after Sunday, they gathered along the steps. Parishioners talked with one another, families connected with other families. But these conversations were muted, as the church's future and past linger in limbo.

German immigrants constructed the facility in 1867, and the ornate organ was installed a decade later. The stained-glass windows were shipped from Bavaria in 1914, and World War I threatened to stall the delivery. The Rev. Aloysius Schmitt served the parish before World War II, and he was stationed at Pearl Harbor when the Japanese attacked. He was honored for saving several soldiers' lives before becoming the first chaplain to die in the war.

These are the stories that will be lost, said parishioner John Nicks. His own grandparents emigrated from Germany, and "when they came to America, they came to St. Mary's," he said. "This church means everything to us," he said. "All we can do now is pray."
And that they did, uniting together as they recited, "Hail Mary, full of grace."

© 2009 *Telegraph Herald*. Reprinted with permission.

THE WITNESS

August 30, 2009   Page 1

Likelihood of parish closing increases: Status of St. Mary's in Dubuque is forwarded to the archbishop.
By Sr. Carol Hoverman, OSF, Editor

Dubuque — This past weekend, parishioners at St. Mary Parish in Dubuque were saddened as their pastor, Father Steven Rosonke, announced with a heavy heart that, after many months of meeting, discussion and prayer, "the Pastoral Council has voted to endorse the recommendation of the Pastoral Planning Committee and the Finance Council to seek closure of the parish."

A letter to that effect has been sent to Archbishop Jerome Hanus, OSB, who will study all the data collected over the past years before making a decision.

A number of factors have led to the local conclusion that the parish is no longer viable — admirable attempts at revitalizing the parish, a decline in parish membership, dwindling contributions and involvement, coupled with current and anticipated debt, and major maintenance costs to parish buildings exceeding $2 million.

Progress reports were made frequently to parishioners through homilies, the parish bulletin, and parish meetings.

Concerns included the difficulty in identifying parishioners to serve on committees and to assist at parish events.

Deteriorating facilities, declining number of baptisms, increasing number of funerals, fewer weddings and new families, and less financial support have all contributed to the recommendation. In recent years, the parish has become heavily reliant upon bequests to meet regular operational costs.

In his homily on Sunday, Father Rosonke emphatically stated that no one on the committee or councils wanted to recommend closure, but members felt they had exhausted every other option.

"We know this is painful for everyone involved," said Travis King, chair of the St. Mary's Finance Council and a member of both the Pastoral Planning Committee and the St. Mary's/St. Patrick's Cluster Council. "But we also want to urge parishioners not to get discouraged with their faith because of our endorsement to recommend closure. We encourage them to continue sharing their gifts to help build up the body of Christ in the Dubuque area, as they move through this difficult process and beyond."

If the archbishop accepts the recommendation, a date will be set for closing and eventually for a final Mass. A committee of parish and archdiocesan representatives, working with civic leaders, will be formed to plan for future use of the parish property.

In the interim, Father Rosonke asked parishioners to be patient with the unfolding process. He acknowledged that closing a parish is like experiencing a death in the family and promised his assistance and that of parish staff members in the days ahead.

"My desire and the desire of the parishioners and the archdiocese is that the historical significance of this church will be preserved, if possible," he said at the end of his homily. "But as important as the future of this church building is, even more important is the welfare of the parishioners in dealing with this loss."

© 2009 *The Witness*. Reprinted with permission.

Sacred Heart
Photo © 2009, Don Long, Jr.

I came to St. Mary's in 1925, when I was six-months-old with my parents, Bernard and Mary (Schaetzle) Vonderheide, and six-year-old brother, Joseph.

I made my First Communion and Confirmation, graduating from grade school and continued on with the Franciscan nuns to the Immaculate Conception Academy. I married Floyd Heying at St. Mary's and was married for 37 years when he passed away. Later I married Bern Hillary at St. Mary's and we've been together 23 years.

Christmas was my favorite Holy Day — seeing the beautiful crib and going to Midnight Mass with my mother. Forty Hours was a beautiful service with all the red roses and our beautiful gold altar. I feel sad to leave St. Mary's after attending the church for 85 years.
—Betty (Vonderheide) Hillary (2010)

Images of the last Christmas Mass celebrated at St. Mary's mingled with memories of Christmas Mass of the past. It was a family tradition, even when we were no longer "actively" practicing the Catholic faith, to attend the Midnight Mass celebrating the birth of our Savior. I cried at the realization that this was the last time I would see the church of my childhood, the church that beckoned me back to the Catholic faith, lit up and decorated in honor of Christ's Mass; the last time I would see the beautiful Nativity scene.
—Candice Chaloupka (2010)

Memory of Easter Service at St. Mary's Church, 2010, and closing tradition of the 'Berberich' tradition.

Memories revisit the 8 a.m. Easter morning Mass: Dad spruced up in his dark gray suit — a distinguished, tall, silver haired gentleman, walking five women down the center aisle; mom, three sisters, and me.

Against a backdrop of gold-leaf ceiling and stained glass windows, an Easter parade to praise the Lord. The pastel colored dresses, hats adorned with tulle ribbon, flowers of poppy orange, canary yellow, or strawberry red, framed a joyous family visiting the Lord in their finest.

As the Alleluias rang, a thankful family praised God, in anticipation of baked ham, buttered mashed potatoes, home canned green beans, highlighted with a white coconut covered bunny cake, complete with jelly bean eyes and licorice whiskers.

In May, the massive doors of a steeple of faith close, embracing the memories of grade school requiem masses, morning novenas, and thoughts of a quiet man of German heritage, who graced our family by walking in the footsteps of Christ. —Connie Berberich Weis (2010)

Sisters of Mt. Saint Francis Say Goodbye

Approximately 90 Franciscan sisters and former teachers gathered at St. Mary's Church on Sunday afternoon, April 18 to celebrate the Franciscan presence in St. Mary's Parish since 1879 through 2010. All of the music used for the service was written by members of the Franciscan community.

Sister Marie Therese Kalb played "The Bells of St. Mary's" as part of the of the celebration of Franciscan presence in St. Mary's Parish since 1879. Sisters Mary Hauber and Mary Terese Kalb both claim St. Mary's as their home parish from which they entered Mount St. Francis.

The closing of St. Mary's is the passing of an era — as people of faith, we don't hold on to anything, but are open to how God is drawing us from the past to the future. My mom taught me that memories are not in a building, they are wherever we go. We carry them in our hearts. As Franciscans we need to be light enough to carry what we have to wherever God is leading us.

Our history tells us a lot about our future — our history has us serving the poor and the immigrants. That is what we continue to do. It is who we are as Franciscans.

There is a place for mourning, but we trust God who is leading us to another place. It is important to mourn what we lose, if we don't grieve we will be angry and that's not helpful to the Christian community. —Sister Nancy Schreck, OSF (2010)

Sister Marie Terese Kalb Plays the Violin
Photo © 2010, Sr. Carol Hoverman, OSF

Sisters Karla Kloft, Cathy Katoski, Donalda Kehoe join in the singing
Photo © 2010, Sr. Carol Hoverman, OSF

Starting on Sunday, May 23, 2010, the Telegraph Herald of Dubuque, Iowa, began a four-part series on the history and closing of St. Mary's Church.

Reporter Mary Nevans-Pederson authored these articles that covered the history of the building and the people, the art and architecture of the church, the fight to save St. Mary's, and the coverage of the final Mass.

TELEGRAPH HERALD

May 23, 2010   Page 16A

Our View: Sad Farewell to St. Mary's

It might seem that there is little left to be said about the imminent closure of St. Mary's Catholic Church in Dubuque. Maybe so. But, yet, some things must be said anyway. Though few can dispute the 21st century realities that brought about the decision to close this tradition-rich parish, the closure is saturated with sadness, nostalgia and, in some cases, even anger.

The history of St. Mary's Church is tightly interwoven with that of Dubuque overall. The parish was more than one denomination. It was more than a church. St. Mary's was a mainstay in one of Dubuque's earliest and significant neighborhoods.

The parish's modest beginnings, its parishioners' remarkable effort to construct a majestic church and its service to generations of Catholics (many of them German immigrants and their descendants) will never be forgotten. It can only be hoped that people will most remember St. Mary's in its best years and decades, and not so much the recent challenges that made the closure necessary.

A parish is not its building. A parish is its people. People to serve on committees, to volunteer their time and talents, and, yes, to fill the collection basket. Over the years, the reality is that St. Mary's lost too much of its human and financial capital to sustain itself as a parish. St. Mary's lacked the numbers, the corps of energized volunteers, and the money to stay in operation.

As the Telegraph Herald series starting today makes clear, St. Mary's Catholic Church leaves an indelible memory in the hearts and minds of thousands upon thousands of Dubuquers. It was more than a place to worship and to receive sacraments. It was community. It will be missed.

Editorials reflect the consensus of the *Telegraph Herald* Editorial Board.

© 2009 *Telegraph Herald*. Reprinted with permission.

Photo © 2010, Sr. Carol Hoverman, OSF

The Last Mass
Photo © 2010, Sr. Carol Hoverman, OSF

Last Mass

On May 25, 2010, St. Mary's Church was packed with people who came to say goodbye. Some were parishioners; some just wanted to take advantage of the last opportunity to see the "finest church west of the Mississippi." Many were life-long members. All shared in the grief and shock that St. Mary's was closing.

Archbishop Jerome Hanus, O.S.B., was the principal celebrant with Reverend Steve Rosonke, Pastor of St. Mary's co-celebrating. The following is a list of the priests who also helped with the celebration of the Mass:

Monsignor James Barta
Monsignor John Friedell
Monsignor Francis Friedl
Monsignor Karl Glovik
Father Clarence Beckley
Father Dwayne Thoman
Father Ardel Barta

Father Steven Lundgren
Father Fred Fangmann
Father William Wilkie
Father Ron Friedell
Father Eugene Kutsch
Father Dan Knepper
Monsignor Richard Funke

Joyce Whelan
Photo © 2010, Digital Dubuque

Father Steve Rosonke and Archbishop Jerome Hanus
Photo © 2010, Digital Dubuque

Gathering Rites

Hymn: *Send Us Your Spirit, #282*

Greeting

Rites of Sprinkling: *River of Glory, #328*

Opening Prayer

Liturgy of the Word

First Reading: *Revelation 21:1-5*

Responsorial Psalm: *Psalm 84*

R: *Blessed are they who dwell in your house, O Lord.*

Gospel Acclamation: *Alleluia*

Gospel: *Luke 1:26-38*

Homily

Celebrating the Mass for the closing of St. Mary's Parish is an occasion for sadness and grieving. In a certain sense, the feelings we have are similar to what we experience at the funeral of a beloved member of the family.

Closing a parish is one of the most difficult things I do as your Archbishop. Even though the whole Archdiocese, along with the entire heartland of America, is undergoing significant downsizing, it is still very difficult.

This is especially true for you who are members of this parish. You have had to endure the slow death of something that is very dear to you. You have worked hard, trying to avert this moment. Many other people have shared your pain, in particular those who had treasured moments of their Catholic faith here at St. Mary's. Many former members have returned in these last weeks; many of you are with us this evening. Your presence and consolation are appreciated.

As we began planning for this event, I was asked to suggest possible choices for the Mass we would celebrate and the readings from the Holy Bible that we would hear. Our desire was to honor the Blessed Virgin Mary, the great patroness of this church.

The Church has given us many titles for Mary. After careful study, I proposed that in this special Mass, we honor the Blessed

Father Steve Rosonke reads the Gospel
Photo © 2010, Digital Dubuque

Archbishop Hanus gives the Homily
Photo © 2010, Digital Dubuque

Virgin Mary as the Temple of the Lord. This title, "Mary, Temple of the Lord," reflects fittingly the history of this community.

When the founders of this parish, in the early 1860s, realized that they needed a larger church to accommodate the rapidly growing community, they thought very boldly. They wanted their new church to be as impressive as the great cathedrals of Europe.

The result is this Temple of the Lord. Here within these walls, they would be able to experience the presence of God. Under this roof, and in the shadow of the impressive steeple, the community would come to worship God. Here they would be instructed by the sacred scriptures and the homilies, sanctified through the sacraments and especially nourished by the Body and Blood of Christ. Here in this temple, Jesus would be present in the Eucharist — present so that young and old, women and men, Sisters and deacons and priests would be able to kneel in adoration. This would truly be a Temple of the Lord.

That is why it was fitting that those pioneers dedicated their church building to Mary, because in a real sense, she is very appropriately given the title, "Temple of the Lord."

We heard in the Gospel passage just proclaimed the familiar story of the Annunciation. God sent the angel Gabriel to Mary. The angel told her, "You will conceive in your womb and bear a son, and you shall name him Jesus."

Mary, not surprisingly, couldn't understand how this would happen. How could she contain within her small body the Almighty God? What human being would presume to become a "Temple of the Lord?"

Of course, this was not the work of a human being. Rather, as the angel explained, it was possible only by grace. Mary heard the reassuring words of the angel, "The Holy Spirit will come upon you, and the power of the Most High will overshadow you." Mary became the Temple of the Lord when she conceived the Son of God and nurtured him in her womb. What she was by the grace of God, this building became for the human community that used it.

But we can go even further. The Christian people not only use holy buildings. By hearing and doing the word of God, they become holy themselves. That is why Christian tradition says that sacred buildings fulfill their purpose when the people who use them become themselves "temples of the Lord."

Saint Paul proclaimed this truth several times. To the Ephesians, he wrote: "You are fellow citizens of the saints and members of God's household, built upon the foundation of the apostles and prophets, Christ Jesus himself being the cornerstone, in whom the whole structure grows into a holy temple in the Lord." (Ephesians 2:19-21)

The founders and all the parishioners who followed them became temples of the Lord because they worshiped and were sanctified within this temple built by human hands. Writing to the Corinthians, Saint Paul asked, "Do you not know that you are God's temple and that God's Spirit dwells in you? ... God's temple is holy, and you are that temple." (I Corinthians 3: 16-17)

That is part of what we are celebrating in this Eucharist. We are thanking God that this parish and these buildings were the significant instruments through which the historic members of this parish were able to be formed into the temple of God — a community of holy ones, of "saints," dedicated to the love of God and the love of neighbor. These buildings were built for this purpose. They served and fulfilled this purpose well. They did it because of their beauty and their usefulness.

All of this was in imitation of Mary, whose faith was crowned in the beauty of her Assumption, pictured in the mural above the altar. What Mary did first and perfectly, St. Mary's Parish strove to imitate and replicate here in the heart of Dubuque.

Those of us living at the beginning of the 21st century are called to live through the downsizing that is characterizing so much of the Midwest. We must do this with hope. Recognizing our sadness and mourning the loss of former arrangements, we believe that Jesus calls us into the future. Jesus calls us to hope.

The first reading of today's Mass expressed this call. Saint John, in the Book of Revelation, shared the vision of the future that the Glorified and Risen Christ gives to his followers.

Recall those words:

I, John, saw a new heaven and a new earth ...
I heard a loud voice from the throne saying,

'Behold … God will dwell with them and they will
be his people
And God himself will always be with them as their God.
God will wipe every tear from their eyes,
And there shall be no more death or mourning, wailing
or pain,
For the old order has passed away.'
The One who sat on the throne said,
'Behold, I make all things new.' (Revelation 21:1-5)
This is the Hope to which we are called.

So, we thank God for all the grace and blessings and accomplishments of the past. I thank each and every one of you for your sharing in the life of this parish and for your support of its programs and facilities. I share your sadness. The members of other parishes also share your grief. You are in the prayers of so many who care and identify with you. Accept from them support; accept welcome into the neighboring parishes which stand ready to receive you into their communities. Take there the many gifts and talents and generosity which God has given you.

Finally, as you enter into the life of your new parishes, open your hearts to the prayer which we used at the beginning of Mass. We prayed:

> Lord God,
> With artistry beyond all telling
> You fashioned a holy temple for your Son
> In the virginal womb of Blessed Mary;
> Grant that, in faithfully safeguarding the grace of our baptism,
> We may worship you in spirit and in truth
> And become like Mary, a temple of your glory.
> We ask this through Christ our Lord. Amen.

Most Rev. Jerome Hanus, OSB, Archbishop of Dubuque
May 25, 2010

Prayer of the Faithful

The Lord's Prayer
Photo © 2010, Digital Dubuque

Eucharistic Prayer
Photo © Digital Dubuque

Liturgy of the Eucharist

Preparation of the Altar and the Gifts

    Gifts carried by Jackie Williams, Annie Wertz, and Sr. Donard Collins, BVM

Hymn: *Hail, Holy Queen, #323*

Eucharistic Prayer

Sung Acclamations: *Mass of Creation, pp 41-42*

Rite of Communion

Lord's Prayer

Sign of Peace

Breaking of the Bread

Communion

Prayer after Communion

Distribution of Communion
Photo © Digital Dubuque

Ritual of Remembering

Presider: *Blessed are you, Emmanuel, God with us. In this place we have come to know and celebrate your love for us, your people. We trust in your providential care for us and your guidance to our true and lasting home. Be with us now and always and so we say, Blessed be God for ever!*

All (sing): *"Blessed be God for ever!"*

At the Ambry:

Presider: We hear the prayers for healing and remember those sick who have come here for comfort, who with the oil of strength have been anointed in this place.
(Pause for silent prayer)
We thank you and we praise you for all who have been anointed in this place. Blessed be God for ever!

All (sing): *"Blessed be God for ever!"*

L: *At the Ambry*, R: *At the Reconciliation Room*
Photo © 2010, Digital Dubuque

At the Shrine of Our Lady of Perpetual Help:
> Presider: Let us remember the generations of prayer and devotion that this sacred image has inspired.
> (Pause for silent prayer).
> We thank you for inspiring true devotion in us here to our patroness, our Blessed Mother Mary. Blessed be God for ever!
>
> All (sing):*"Blessed be God for ever!"*

At the Reconciliation Room:
> Presider: Let us remember the times we have been forgiven, comforted, consoled in the Sacrament of Penance. (Pause for silent prayer).
> We thank you and we praise you for the healing and reconciling love that has been given through the Sacrament of Penance in this church.
> Blessed be God for ever!"
>
> All (sing):*"Blessed be God for ever!"*

At the Font:
> Presider: Let us remember the baptisms celebrated here. (Pause for silent prayer). We remember the sound of flowing water; we hear "I baptize you in the name of the Father, and of the Son, and of the Holy Spirit." We hold in our hearts those whom we have welcomed into the Body of Christ in this place.
> We thank you and we praise you for the life of faith for all who have passed through the waters of new life at this font. Blessed be God for ever!
>
> All (sing):*"Blessed be God for ever!"*

At the Ambo:

> Presider: Let us remember the power of God's word proclaimed here in scripture and in preaching. (Pause for silent prayer). We thank you and we praise you for your holy Word proclaimed here in faith and preached here in sincerity.
> May it echo always in our hearts.
> Blessed be God for ever!
>
> All (sing): *"Blessed be God for ever!"*

At the Altar:

> Presider: Let us remember the times we have gathered for the sacred banquet:
> the Triduum kept each year,
> the Sundays on which we worshipped faithfully,
> the first communion celebrations,
> the feast days of saints and martyrs,
> the marriages witnessed here,
> the funerals held here in hope.
> Let us pray.
> (Pause for silence)
> God our refuge, our home is in you.
> You are greater than any temple, church or cathedral that can be built by human hands, yet in this place we have met your divine presence. This church building has been a place of blessing for us. Protect us on our way. Lead us to a new assembly of your faithful people. We ask this through Christ our Lord.
>
> All: *Amen*

Concluding Rites

Final Blessing
Dismissal
Final Hymn: *Holy God, We Praise Thy Name,* #365

The choir sang beautifully joined by the voices of the congregants. All were invited to a reception following the Mass in the Parish Hall.

For the last time as St. Mary's Parish, the song, *Bells of St. Mary,* were played at St. Mary's Church.

Prior to the dismissal, Archbishop Jerome Hanus, OSB, read the decree officially closing St. Mary's Church.

Sister Marie Therese Kalb, OSF
Photo © 2010, Digital Dubuque

Go in Peace
Photo © 2010, Digital Dubuque

Jerome Hanus, O.S.B., By the Grace of God and Favor of the Apostolic See Archbishop of Dubuque
DECREE
Regarding St. Mary's Parish, Dubuque, Iowa

St. Mary's Parish came into being in response to a petition of German families to Bishop Loras in 1849 for a parish to provide for the German-speaking Catholics of Dubuque. Thus began the history of a proud community where for more than a century-and-a-half, the Catholic faithful heard the Word of God proclaimed, were formed and educated in Catholic teaching, participated in the Eucharistic Sacrifice, and received the Sacraments of the Church. The community over the years contributed greatly to the social fabric of Dubuque and preserved elements of a German and Catholic heritage through times of both prosperity and economic distress.

The first church building, dedicated to the Holy Trinity, was constructed of stone in 1850 on the corner of 8th and White Streets. Because of rapid growth, the present much larger church was completed in 1867 at the corner of 15th and White Streets. It was named St. Mary's under the title of her Assumption. Over the years many improvements were made, but the building also suffered a serious fire in 1976, and continuing deterioration caused by normal aging.

Pastoral leadership over the decades was provided by more than a dozen priests and by two pastoral administrators from the diaconal community. The families of the parish offered many of their children to the service of God as priests and religious-more than thirty priests, nearly seventy sisters, and seven brothers.

Providing Catholic education for the young was a high priority. The first classes, in 1851, were conducted in the basement of the old church. Classes were moved to 15th Street when in 1870 the parish built the convent, now Maria House. Various other buildings were used over the years. Initially, teachers were laymen, then the Sisters of Charity of the Blessed Virgin Mary (Dubuque), and the La Crosse Franciscans. The Dubuque Franciscans began their decades-long service in 1879.

A high school for boys, with the Brothers of Mary as teachers, operated from 1907 to 1929. High school girls were educated in the nearby Immaculate Conception Academy (on 17th Street) until it was transferred to Davis Street, now Shalom Retreat Center.

The Casino Building, constructed in 1900 as a center for social and recreational activities, was significantly modified in 1950 to provide more classrooms and other rooms for fostering community. St. Mary's was a founding parish of Wahlert High School in 1959.

With the decline in enrollment that took place in the 1970s, St. Mary's consolidated with St. Patrick's in 1982 as Downtown Catholic. It changed its name to St. Mary's/St. Patrick's School in 1988. It became part of the consolidated Holy Family Catholic School System in 2001 along with the other parishes in the city. As enrollment continued to decline, St. Mary's/St. Patrick's became part of St. Francis Consolidated School in 2003, serving the families of St. Mary, St. Patrick, Sacred Heart, and Holy Trinity. St. Francis closed in 2005. Currently families of St. Mary's are encouraged to enroll their children in Holy Ghost Elementary School, Mazzuchelli Catholic Middle School, and Wahlert Catholic High School.

St. Mary's and St. Patrick's were placed under a unified leadership in 2000, with Deacon Timothy LoBianco serving as pastoral administrator.

After much planning and several attempts at revitalization, it gradually became clear to church leadership and much of the membership that the parish was no longer sustainable. In the summer of 2009, the pastor, along with the lay directors, having discussed the matter for several months and having received the support of the Pastoral Planning Committee and the Finance Council, endorsed the proposal to seek closure of the parish. As Archbishop, I concluded that it was necessary to approve this request.

Therefore, on September 14, 2009, in accord with canon 515, §2 of the Code a/Canon Law, I sought the advice of the Council of Priests. Having heard the Council's advice and having continued to reflect on the situation and to receive the advice of the Episcopal vicar, the pastor, and the special planning committee, I have decided that reluctantly the decision must be finalized. By this decree, according to Church Law ("Paroecias ... supprimere"), I officially close St. Mary Parish, Dubuque, Iowa, effective May 25, 2010.

All registers containing records of baptism, confirmation, marriage, and burials hitherto preserved by St. Mary Parish are to be conveyed to St. Raphael Parish, Dubuque, where they are to be faithfully preserved according to canon 535, §§1-5.

Since St. Mary's was established as a national parish to serve the German-speaking people of the area, no territorial boundaries are affected. Parishioners of St. Mary Parish are free to become members of any parish in the area. The respective parishes will assume the pastoral care of these parishioners.

Because of accumulated debts, any assets of St. Mary Parish will first be used to pay off these debts. Remaining assets will follow the parishioners to their new parishes according to the different percentages of those transferring membership. The number of those who were parishioners on January 1, 2009, who have registered at different parishes by December 31, 2010, will determine percentages. All juridical transactions will be cared for by the civil corporation of St. Mary's Church, in accord with the laws of the Church and of the State of Iowa.

Promulgation of this Decree is to be made in a public fashion as determined by the pastor and lay directors of St. Mary Parish. Any proposed petition against this Decree is to be made in writing to my office in not more than ten useful days from the date of promulgation.

Given at Dubuque, Iowa, on this 25th day of May, 2010.
+ Most Rev. Jerome Hanus, O.S.B., Archbishop of Dubuque
Betty Schuell, Chancellor

The Gathering

Many families stayed behind in the church to say their last good-byes, share memories, take pictures, and attend the gathering that was held in the basement of the church; all were invited.

Postscript

As of this writing, it is unknown what will happen to the buildings and the beautiful works of art contained within. Theresa Crabill started a website and petition urging the

Archdiocese to invite an outside organization to assume responsibility for the church.

One such organization Ms. Crabill suggested was the Institute of Christ the King Sovereign Priest; an organization that "does its own fundraising, brings its own priests, operates independently, but within the archdiocese, and strictly follows the archbishop's orders." (www.savestmarydbq.com)

Archbishop Hanus has made contact with the Institute to get more information, but by the time this book went to press, he had not received a reply.

Gathering
Photo © 2010, Candice Chaloupka

Empty Pews
Photo © 2010, Candice Chaloupka

As a former member of St. Mary's, I hope and pray whatever happens to the building that was St. Mary's Church, that God is honored. I can only continue to trust in God and that "all things work for good for those who love God." (Romans 8:28, NAB)
—Candice Chaloupka

The Bells of St. Mary's toll and will ring out no more.
—Al Hetizman (2010)

Empty Chair
Photo © 2010, Candice Chaloupka

St. Mary's Last Mass—A Personal Reflection
By Melissa King

It's like mourning the loss of a loved one. The words float from the Altar through the cathedral ceilings and touch the ears of the packed St. Mary's Church. Our last Mass. I hold my second-born baby girl, as I sit next to my husband and older daughter Erin. As Archbishop Hanus prays over the sacramental locations of church, a tear escapes down my face as memories of how it all began run through my head.

I started attending St. Mary's in 2004, just after I met my would-be husband. I wasn't Catholic, but Travis was, and he invited me to join him. Every Sunday, I would enjoy going. I loved the traditions and the people. It was Father Barta's personable and friendly demeanor that started me going to RCIA classes.

Later that year, during the Easter season, I was sealed with the gift of the Holy Spirit in Confirmation, received Christ in my First Communion, and was fully welcomed into the Catholic faith and the St. Mary's family. It was not long after that I was proclaiming God's words from the Ambo. After 25 years, I felt at home, and God had welcomed me into his house.

That August, Travis and I were engaged. Being married at St. Mary's was our first and only choice.

The year after, August 12, 2006, I donned the white dress. As I walked the long red aisle of St. Mary's on the arm of my father on my way to meet my husband at the Altar, the paintings of angels watched overhead. I remember the look on Travis's face as joyous tears rolled down his cheeks while he made his covenant to me before God. It was a beautifully faith-filled ceremony, and I truly felt God's grace bestowed on our marriage that day.

It was slightly over a year later that we would once again stand in front of God's Altar with the statues of Mary and Jesus watching overhead. This time, a tiny baby girl, our first born Erin, was wearing a white dress

— *made from my wedding gown that had knelt here the year before. Quietly sleeping, the water rolled off her head, washing clean the sins of her world. She stirred only when the parishioners' joyous claps welcomed their newest and youngest member into our parish. Equipped with the light of Christ, she would start her journey of faith that September day.*

I took God's gifts and my enthusiasm and joined the Religious Education teaching team. That year, I guided 17 St. Mary/St. Pat students to discover what I had discovered just a few years prior. I showed them God's great mysteries and his power of forgiveness. They showed me the future of the Church, and I was proud to see them experience God in a new way through their First Communion.

With family so far away, St. Mary's was our family. We shared each other's joys and sorrows, prayed together for God to help the sorrowful, and thanked Him for His many blessings. I was excited to see everyone every Sunday, and worried whenever some of my older friends were not there.

We were overjoyed to announce to our faith family that we would be expecting baby number two the summer Erin turned two. But it would be the month before we would welcome Anna into the world that my husband, who tirelessly over the years tried to keep our church afloat, would stand before us and announce with heavy heart that our beloved St. Mary's would need to close her doors.

I thought I would be prepared for this day — the final Mass, or so I thought. I am not sure I understood until today what this church meant to me. I am not sure that I understood what Church really was. My husband had told me that it is the people that make up Christ's Church, not the building. Today, I get it.

Today, I stand with Christ's Church, his family gathered before him, mourning our loss. For the family that gathered here together for so many Sundays, it will never be the same.

We will no longer be able to share our lives, our faith and our blessings all together as one, soon to be scattered amongst other parishes like leaves in the wind. My daughters will not be able to visit the place their parents married, where our family started, where they stared their journey of faith. They will not be able to bring their husbands or children to this place of worship to show them St. Mary's wonderful faith community.

I am overwhelmed with emotion, trying so hard to hold back the tears and be strong. Welling up in my eyes, tears can no longer be contained and stream down my face in a flood as Sister Carol plays The Bells of St. Mary's *one last time. I close my eyes and pray for God's peace.*

Wedding of Travis and Melissa King, 2006
Contributed by King Family

Amelia Schneider
Photo Contributed by Kirschbaum/Ralph Family

The Founding Families

A debt of gratitude is owed to the founding members of St. Mary's, as well as to those who went on to faithfully serve the church and community through their membership.

The following are the families listed in the Church Archives as belonging to the parish when St. Mary's was built.

Albinger, William
Altman, Theodore, wife Mary, sons Frank and Peter
Bassler, Benedict
Baule, Henry Joseph, wife Maggie
Bauman, Charles
Bauer, Mr. and Mrs. Andrew
Bauer, Albinus
Baumhover, Bernard and Mary and daughter
Baumhover, Anton and Ann, sons Louis and Frank
Beaver, Mr. and Mrs. Mathias, sons Paul, John, and daughter
Beck, Nick and Daughter
Becker, Bernard and Katharine, a son, two daughters

Becker, Mr. and Mrs. Gerhardt, Anton and Jr.
Becker, Bernard, and Katharine, a son, two daughters
Becker, Mr. and Mrs. Gerhardt, Anton and Jr.
Becker, Mr. and Mrs. Jacob
Engelbert, Mathias and Helena, son Miles, daughters Mary, and Kate
Hessling, Han and 3 sons
Millerleide, Mr. and Mrs. John B., son John
Nagele, Tony and Frank
Nagelmaker, Mr. and Mrs. Henry
Neumann, Charles and Caroline, sons Otto and Albert, daughter Bertha
Nicks, Mr. and Mrs. Peter or Nicholas, son Nick
Nickels, Domenick, Elizabeth, daughters Kate, Mary, Emma, Alois
Nipp, Nick and Theresa
Oeth, Andrew
Oeth, Peter and Catherine, son Frank
Oser, Valentine
Ott, Mr. and Mrs. Joseph, son Joe
Pals, Mr. and Mrs. Peter, sons Nick, John, daughters Elizabeth, and Margaret
Palen, Nick and Barbara, son Nick, daughter Mary
Pauw, Mr. and Mrs. Frank
Pfiffner, Mr. and Mrs. Jacob Sr., son Andrew and wife
Pfiffner, Anton and Margaret
Pfiffner, Jacob and Katherine Jr.
Pfoltzer, Mrs. Henry, daughters Josephene and Mary
Phillips, Frank and Theresa
Piekenbrock, Mr. and Mrs. Eberhardt
Pillmeier, John and Anna, sons John and Joseph, daughter Kate
Pregler, Mr. and Mrs. John, son John
Raesle, Mr. and Mrs. Anton, sons John and Anton, daughter Mary
Reich, Mr. and Mrs. Christ
Reichman, Alex and John
Reiger, sons Joseph and George

Reinfried, Mr. and Mrs. Frank, sons Frank and Joseph
Renie, Phillip and Mary
Rhomberg, Mr. and Mrs. Joseph, sons Joseph and Alvin
Rhomberg, Mr. and Mrs. Dominick
Ritshatch, Mr. and Mrs. Mary, sons Joseph and Edward
Roedler, Mr. and Mrs., son Louis and a daughter
Roepsch, Mr. and Mrs. George Sr.
Roesner, Jake and Mary Sr., son Jake, daughter Anna
Roth, William
Rottler, Mr. and Mrs. Anton, son John, daughter Anna Margaret
Rubeck, Mr. and Mrs. George, son George, daughters Lena, Barbara and Anna
Rubeck, Mr. and Mrs. Peter
Rugamer, Mr. and Mrs. John, son Peter
Sahm, Peter and Rose
Sandt, Mr. and Mrs. Philip
Sauer, Valentine and Elizabeth
Sauerwein, Joseph and Anna, daughters Gertrude and Barbara
Schard, Mr. and Mrs. John, son Peter and wife, son John
Schafer, Mary
Schmit, Mr. and Mrs. P., son Nick
Schmit, Mr. and Mrs. John, son John, daughters Kate and Mary
Schmitz, John
Schneider, Gotlieb, wife Amelia, son, Emil, daughter Minnie
Scheneberger, Mr. and Mrs. Jacob, son Jacob, daughters Kate and Louisa
Schoetzle, George
Schroeder, Mr. and Mrs. Nichols, sons Frank and Peter
Schroeman, Nick and Elizabeth, son John
Schrup, Mr. and Mrs. John, sons Theodore, Robert and Peter, daughter Kate
Schuler, Peter and Anna
Schuler, Mr. and Mrs. John
Schulte, Bernard and Anna, son John

Seeberger, Mr. and Mrs. Jacob, 2 sons
Seeger, Ignatz and Gertrude
Seaman, Peter
Seidel, Anton and Aceclete
Seitz, Mr. and Mrs. Peter, sons Ferdinand and Ernst, daughter Lena
Spahn, Mr. and Mrs., sons John and Frank
Specht, Mr. and Mrs. Peter
Stammeyer, Mr. and Mrs. Joseph, son John
Stammeyer, Mr. and Mrs. Peter, daughter Kate
Stem, Joseph
Stieber, Frank and family
Steines, Mr. and Mrs. Anton, 3 daughters
Stirn, John and Mary, son Frank and daughter Mary
Stolteben, William and Mary, sons Rudolph and Tony
Stolteben, Mr. and Mrs. Anton, son William, daughters Bertha
    and Clara
Streinz, Andrew
Strudeman, George, son Barney
Strueber, Christian and Pauline, sons Frank, John and Ernest,
    four daughters
Sustman Mr. and Mrs., sons Tony and John
Theis, Mr. and Mrs. Nick, son Nick
Thomas, Mr. and Mrs. Charles, son Charles, daughter Caroline
Traut, Mr. and Mrs. Joseph, sons Paul, Jacob and Joseph,
    daughter Mary
Trexler, Mr. and Mrs. John, sons John and Adolph, daughters Caroline,
    Catharine and Clara
Trieb, Mr. and Mrs. Jacob, son Joseph
Tschirgi, Mathias and Catharine, son John
Tschudi, Joseph and Elizabeth, sons Fred and Joseph, daughter Kate
VanDuehlman, John and Henrietta, son Tony, daughter Mary
VanHalter, Mr. and Mrs. Andrew, sons Anton and John, daughter
Voelker, Mr. and Mrs. Leopold, sons Christ, Andrew, John,
    daughters Kate, Mary, Lizzy, Lena

Vogel, Adam and Emma

Vogel, Mr. and Mrs. George

Vogel, Mr. and Mrs. Peter

Vogenthaler, Peter or Andrew and Ann, sons Peter and Joseph

Vombacher, Adam

Walter, Mr. and Mrs. Rochus, sons Asa, Andrew, and Albert, daughters Mary and Josephine

Welter, Henry and Kate, daughter Louisa

Welter, Peter and Rose

Welty, Joseph or John and Mary, sons Joseph and Jacob

Werner, M. and Clara, daughter Lena

Weitz, Peter

Wernimont, Mr. and Mrs. Nick, sons Nick and George

Wertin, Peter and Mary, son Peter, daughter Theresa

Westercamp, John and Mary, son Barney

Willging, Mr. and Mrs. George, sons Henry, George, William, Frank and Edward, daughter Kate

Wilke, Peter and Mike

Wilke, Casper

Winter, Peter and Kate

Wirtz, Mr. and Mrs. Christ, sons Henry and Christ

Witmer, Mr. and Mrs. Joseph, son Joseph, daughter Bertholda

Witmer, Mrs. John, daughter Elizabeth

Witmer, Mr. and Mrs. John, 2 sons

Zachina, Wenzel and Mary, son John

Zugenbuehler, Mr. and Mrs. Joseph, sons Joseph and Tony, daughters Mary and Kate

(Contributed by St. Mary's Archives)

A listing of the final membership of St. Mary's was not available for printing to respect the privacy of the members.

A Beautifully Carved Pew
Photo © 2009, Don Long, Jr.

Pew Rent

During the 19th and early 20th centuries, one method a church had of collecting money needed for maintenance of the church was through a "Pew Rent."

> *I remember my folks talking about pew rent but we contributed using envelopes. Even the children had envelopes.*
> —Sister Marie Therese Kalb (2010)

> *We had to pay a certain amount to "rent" a pew and your pew was marked. If you did not rent a pew you had to sit in the pews that were marked "free."* —Sister Corinne Kutsch (2010)

The following are letters from the St. Mary's Church Archives concerning pew rent. After the 1920s information on pew rent could not be found and it is assumed the practiced ended around that time. (All the information is typed exactly as it appeared in the original documents, typos and all!)

Some Reasons Why You Should Have a Seat in Your Parish Church

1. By having one or more seats in a Catholic church, you honor God in the up keep of His Home. You love a beautiful home; so does our Lord. Help to make it a respectable place for Him.

2. You thereby prove yourself a member of good standing in your parish. Members of societies must be in good standing. Why not in your parish?

3. No one will then speak uncharitably of you. Did someone else ever take your place in a train? Evidently you did not like it. Neither do renters of a seat in church.

4. You thus help to bear a burden which others have been carrying alone. Any assistance given you in affairs of daily life is appreciated. So also does the renter of a seat value your cooperation in bearing parish burdens.

5. You know you have a contract with the parish. The Church contracts to assist you spiritually, and you agree to support it financially. Now even common law disowns a one-sided contract. You admit that the parish gives you its best service. Would it be fair not to carry out your part of the contract?

6. Your renting of a seat may be somewhat of a hardship. (Permit us fully to assure you that those unable to do so will be given one free). But remember that the support of any organization demands sacrifice. And sacrifice spells esteem and appreciation for the object demanding it. Hence the sacrifices you voluntarily make for your church may be taken as a safe standard for gaging your interest therein.

Dear Reader: Don't you think the various reasons adduced above have a truthful and convincing ring to them? We are sure that you agree with us that they have. Let us all then generously unite in bearing the expense involved in maintaining our seven buildings. We will thereby be brought into closer union with one another, and the sacrifices involved will tend to strengthen and increase our love and friendship of God, the Giver of all good gifts.

Rent Costs

Price given is for whole pew at 5:30, 8:00, 10:00 o'clock Masses.

For 6:45 and 9:00 o'clock Masses, $3 a seat.
Seats in gallery, $2.

Those who do not rent seats should give ten cents for seat if they can. This is for upkeep of church, heat, light, etc. Those unable to pay will be assigned sittings free of charge.

Statement of Pew Rent
January 1, 1919 to July 1, 1919

The renting of the pews January 5th was finished in about fifteen minutes. This time may be shortened still more, if in future, one person in each pew will have the leaflet with the names of all holding sittings in that pew and the money ready when the collectors reach them.

Of course, the names of the old faithful again appear and several new ones, in all a few more than five hundred names. But with fully seven hundred families in the parish, besides many other wage earning individuals, it is evident that this list of honor should be much larger. (Those unable to pay are always assured free sittings).

So far, however, only nine refuse to contribute towards the monthly collections lately introduced (a number who had been overlooked voluntarily brought their offerings) so that at present there can be but very few, if any, who contribute nothing at all for God's cause.

That surely is gratifying and gives reasons to hope that soon the pew rent list will grow to be a complete parish list. God bless the benefactors of church and school.

```
Pew Rent collected:
  1903 — $4,746.25
  1912 — $5,104.40
  1920 — $5,443.64
```

The following is a letter from the St. Mary's Church Archives asking for donations for the Diamond Jubilee and to help reduce church debt. (All the information is typed exactly as it appeared in the original documents, typos and all!)

Sister Mary Theodore,
St. Francis Convent,
Dubuque, Iowa.

February 1, 1927

Dear Friend,
    Do you recall the days when you were a member of St. Mary's parish in Dubuque? When you listened for the chimes from the tall spire and the mellow Angelus at dawn? How grateful you were for the sublime services solemnized under the arched roof of beautiful St. Mary's. What a thrill of joy possessed you when you beheld the gold-leaf frescoes garlanding the walls and the vari-colored lights in the storied windows. You were proud of St. Mary's because its stained glass, its paintings and its altars were the realization of a parish's desire to beautify God's house — the house where you first received the Sacraments and attended Holy Mass. Your efforts and your sacrifices helped every project in the days when St. Mary's peal of bells summoned you to prayer.

As in the days of old, St. Mary's rings a spiritual appeal from its tower beckoning heavenward. You are no longer within hearing but the knell of the year 1927 has so particular an appeal that it reaches out to every heart it once claimed. St. Mary's this year announces its Diamond Jubilee. Across the States it rings that all may know of its coming Consecration.

St. Mary's house have been all these years in debt. A final effort to lift the debt is about to be made. The plan is a special Pre-Lenten Festival to be held February 21-27. A novel feature of this festival will be a "Former Parishioner's Booth." In this booth are to be displayed the gifts that old friends bestow to help wipe out a debt and consecrate a church — a church dear to the hearts of all its former members. Because the privilege of membership was yours, it is fitting that you should share in the honor of the church's consecration and in the spiritual benefits derived therefrom.

We are sincerely hoping that spring will find our beloved St. Mary's clear of debt; that a true Jubilee of Consecration will crown all the works of its many members. Don't you wish to participate in this event? Any donation, cash or bazaar article will be appreciated.

For your material gift be sure that St. Mary's will return spiritual favors a hundred-fold.

Sincerely and gratefully yours,
                        St. Mary's Parish

P.S. Kindly address your reply to,
    Hattie Huber, Dubuque, Ia.

Photo © 2010, Digital Dubuque

Bibliography

Books

Bowerman, Biays. *Saint Patrick Church: Sesquicentennial History, 1853-2003*. Dubuque, IA, 2004.

Crane, Florence. *The Catholic History of Dubuque*. Dubuque, IA: Enterprise Press, 1905.

Hoffmann, Rev. M.M., Ed. *Centennial History of the Archdiocese of Dubuque*. Columbia College Press, 1938.

New American Bible. World Publishing Inc. 1987.

Sigwarth, Anthony. *St. Mary's Church Centennial Brochure*. 1967.

St. Mary's Church Archives

1918 Directory of St. Mary's Catholic Church.

1986 Directory of St. Mary's Catholic Church.

Newspaper article, source unknown. *Silent Classroom.* 1959.

Author unknown. *St. Mary Church Brochure.* 2007.

Interview of Albert Neuman (born 1858) recorded by Peter Hoffman. September 27, 1943.

St. Mary's History. August 1, 1976.

St. Mary's Church Brochure. October 7, 1962.

Schroeder, Karl G. *History of St. Mary's.* November 20, 1935.

Zeyen, Joseph J. *The Assumption.* 1943.

Websites

www.americaslibrary.com

www.ask.com/wiki/Our_Lady_of_Perpetual_Help

www.biblegateway.com

louisville-catholic.net *F.X. Zettler & The Royal Bavarian Art Institute: Crafters of St. Martin's Windows.* (Access date: May 12, 2010)

www.marys-touch.com/history/olhelp.htm

www.savestmarydbq.com

Sponsors

The following pages are dedicated to the businesses and individuals who graciously provided financial or other support so this book could be created.

Jim and Kathy Conlon

Behr's Funeral Home

Don Long, Jr.

Barb Ehlers

St. Mary's Church

The glory, history, and beauty of *St. Mary's* will be cherished forever. The faith, works, and commitment of the congregation will live on through the generations who were blessed to be part of its community.

American Trust
Member FDIC
Simply better banking.

563.582.1841 | Since 1911 | americantrust.com

Because He Came, BHC Publishing was created.
Because He Called, the book was made.
Because He Creates, future books will be published.

BHC Publishing produces both Christian and secular books.

Suzanne Wright & Candice Chaloupka
BHCPublishing@gmail.com
563-451-7914

www.ingramcontent.com/pod-product-compliance
Lightning Source LLC
Chambersburg PA
CBHW042056290426
44112CB00001B/2